Sexualising Society

Series Editor: Cara Acred

Volume 238

Independence Educational Publishers

First published by Independence Educational Publishers

The Studio, High Green

Great Shelford

Cambridge CB22 5EG

England

© Independence 2013

British Library Cataloguing in Publication Data

Sexualising society. -- (Issues ; v. 238)

1. Children and sex. 2. Sex in mass media. 3. Mass media
and children. 4. Social perception in children.
5. Children--Social conditions--21st century.
6. Children--Social life and customs--21st century.

I. Series II. Acred, Cara.

305.2'3'09051-dc23

ISBN-13: 9781861686367

Printed in Great Britain

MWL Print Group Ltd

Contents

Introduction

Sexualising Society is Volume 238 in the **_ISSUES_** series. The aim of the series is to offer current, diverse information about important issues in our world, from a UK perspective.

ABOUT SEXUALISING SOCIETY

Whatever happened to letting children be children? Adults are becoming increasingly worried that society's young people are being subjected to premature sexualisation by the media and the environment around them. With over one in five children in the UK viewing 'inappropriate' content on their smartphones, this seems a legitimate concern. But are we overreacting? This book explores the idea of sexualisation, the impact of porn and the media, and asks what part parents have to play in these issues.

OUR SOURCES

Titles in the **_ISSUES_** series are designed to function as educational resource books, providing a balanced overview of a specific subject.

The information in our books is comprised of facts, articles and opinions from many different sources, including:

- Newspaper reports and opinion pieces
- Website fact sheets
- Magazine and journal articles
- Statistics and surveys
- Government reports
- Literature from special interest groups

A NOTE ON CRITICAL EVALUATION

Because the information reprinted here is from a number of different sources, readers should bear in mind the origin of the text and whether the source is likely to have a particular bias when presenting information (or when conducting their research). It is hoped that, as you read about the many aspects of the issues explored in this book, you will critically evaluate the information presented.

It is important that you decide whether you are being presented with facts or opinions. Does the writer give a biased or unbiased report? If an opinion is being expressed, do you agree with the writer? Is there potential bias to the 'facts' or statistics behind an article?

ASSIGNMENTS

In the back of this book, you will find a selection of assignments designed to help you engage with the articles you have been reading and to explore your own opinions. Some tasks will take longer than others and there is a mixture of design, writing and research based activities that you can complete alone or in a group.

FURTHER RESEARCH

At the end of each article we have listed its source and a website that you can visit if you would like to conduct your own research. Please remember to critically evaluate any sources that you consult and consider whether the information you are viewing is accurate and unbiased.

Pleasure vs profit

Information from Women's Support Project.

What is sexualisation?

In 2007 the American Psychological Association (APA) carried out an extensive review of the impact of sexualisation on young girls. The APA's taskforce provides the following definition of sexualisation as occurring when:

⇨ a person's value comes only from his or her sexual appeal or behaviour, to the exclusion of other characteristics

⇨ a person is held to a standard that equates physical attractiveness with being sexy

⇨ a person is sexually objectified and made into a thing for others' sexual use rather than seen as a person with the capacity for independent action and decision making

⇨ sexuality is inappropriately imposed upon a person.

'Report of the APA Task Force on the Sexualisation of Girls.' American Psychological Association. Zurbriggen et al. (2007) http://www.apa.org/pi/wpo/sexualization.html

Why is it happening?

'We know from our research that commercial pressures towards premature sexualisation and unprincipled advertising are damaging children's well-being. The evidence shows that adults feel children are more materialistic than in past generations, while children themselves feel under pressure to keep up with the latest trends.'

Penny Nicholls, director of children and young people at The Children's Society. http://news.bbc.co.uk/1/hi/uk/8619329.stm

'Though it may not be right, again it wouldn't be the first time a retailer saw a marketing opportunity and jumped... seizing an opportunity. Parents hold the buying power in their wallets.'

Lydia Dishman – http://www.bnet.com/blog/publishing-style/abercrombiespadded-bikinis-for-tweens-prove-theres-nothing-new-under-the-retail-sun/1609

How is it happening?

'How have sex, sexiness and sexualisation gained such favour in recent years as to be the measure by which women's and girls' worth is judged? While it is not a new phenomenon by any means, there is something different about the way it occurs today and how it impacts on younger and younger girls.'

McLellan, 'Sexualised and Trivialized – Making Equality Impossible'. Quoted in 'Getting Real', Tankard Reist (2010)

Researchers looked at 15 websites of popular clothing stores, ranging from bargain to high-end sectors of the junior US market. Clothing was rated according to whether it had only child-like characteristics, revealed or emphasised an intimate body part, or had characteristics that were associated with sexiness.

⇨ 69% of the clothing assessed in the study had only child-like characteristics

⇨ 4% had only sexualising characteristics, while

⇨ 25% had both sexualising and child-like characteristics

⇨ 1% had neither sexualised nor child-like characteristics.

Goodin S et al. (2011). 'Putting On Sexiness: a content analysis of the presence of sexualizing characteristics in girls' clothing.' Sex Roles; DOI:10.1007/s11199-011-9966-8 (c) 2011 AFP

'Boys don't have to look hard for examples of the tough guy in popular culture – he is seen all over the television dial, in advertising, and in the books based on popular TV series. He is held up as a sort of ideal (in sharp contrast to "wimpy" smart guy characters) and he teaches boys that success comes from being aggressive. Increasingly, the influence of this character can be seen in boys' clothing. As the examples below demonstrate, scary imagery, with its undertones of aggression, appears on clothing marketed to boys aged one and up.'

http://www.achilleseffect.com/2011/01/boys-clothing-valuing-toughness-andaggression/

'Fashions like these dovetail perfectly with the messages delivered by film, television, books, and toy advertising, telling boys on the one hand that aggression and toughness are cool and, on the other, that rowdiness and bad behaviour are funny and even expected from boys.'

http://www.achilleseffect.com/2011/01/boys%E2%80%99-clothing-part-2%E2%80%94the-brat/

What are the impacts?

'It is important to analyse cultural representations of gender roles, sexuality and relationships and ask what specific values are being promoted and if these are having a negative impact on child development. Key questions include the impact on children... of stereotyped images of passivity and sexual objectification... the long-term impacts of early exposure to adult sexual themes and the ways in which cultural exposure impacts on parents' roles in protecting and educating children around sexuality in a developmentally appropriate way.'

Newman, 'The Psychological and Developmental Impact of Sexualisation on Children'. Quoted in 'Getting Real' Tankard Reist (2010)

'When girls are dressed to resemble adult women... adults may project adult motives as well as an adult level of responsibility and agency on girls. Images of precocious sexuality in girls may serve to normalize abusive practices such as child abuse, child prostitution, and the sexual trafficking of children... the sexualisation of girls may also contribute to a market for sex with children through the cultivation of new desires and experiences.'

American Psychological Association Taskforce on the Sexualisation of Girls reported in 2007:p 35

'When we allow our young girls' childhood to be about being sexy, we take their attention away from developing their true sense of self and how they can affect the world and we put it on what others want them to be and what the world demands of them.'

http://www.drrobynsilverman.com/body-image/tarty-toys-for-tots-a-pound-of-flesh-too-much-or-much-ado-about-nothing/

'It can be tempting to think that girls are taking the brunt, that boys have it easier. But in some ways the messages we are sending out to boys are just as limiting and restrictive: be macho, be strong, don't show your emotions. Hyper-sexualisation of femininity cannot exist without hypermasculinisation of males. They feed off and reinforce each other.'

Dr Linda Papadopoulos, Sexualisation Review 2010

⇨ The above information is reprinted with kind permission from Women's Support Project. Please visit www.womenssupportproject.co.uk for further information on this subject.

© Women's Support Project

War against the sexualisation of childhood

With girls admitting to dressing and acting in a sexualised way to 'build their brand' and a mobile stock of porn serving as a status symbol for boys, parents and teachers fear that innocence is under attack.

By Julia Belgutay

The figures make chilling reading for parents and teachers alike. More than a quarter of 13-to 15-year-olds in the UK have received sexually explicit text messages, while one in ten children aged ten to 12 and a quarter of 13 to 15-year-olds say they have seen sexually explicit images on the Internet, according to a survey for the charities Family Lives and Drinkaware, which was published last month.

Shocking as these figures may seem, they nevertheless confirm a development that has concerned educationists and parents for some time: the accelerating sexualisation of young children in society.

Earlier this year, Reg Bailey, chief executive of the Mothers' Union charity, led an independent review for the Westminster Government into the commercialisation and sexualisation of childhood.

It highlighted parents' increasing worries about the lack of control they have over the sexualised environment to which their children are exposed. Parents, carers and professionals working with children were particularly concerned about sexually explicit music videos, outdoor adverts containing sexualised images, sexualised clothes and products aimed at young children, and the sexual content in family television programmes, said Mr Bailey.

Judging by media coverage in recent years, the most visible manifestation of the sexualisation and objectification of children has been the emergence of sexualised goods aimed at a young audience.

Retailers and even supermarkets have been condemned for selling padded bras and bikinis, animal-print hot pants, and even pole-dancing kits targeting children of primary school age.

Policy makers in Scotland were so concerned by this development that last year the Scottish Parliament's Equal Opportunities Committee commissioned a team of academics to assess the prevalence of such goods and the views of young people and their carers on their message and impact.

Young people, the authors found, were adamant they made their purchasing decisions for a variety of reasons, including comfort, fashion consciousness and parental input – not simply out of a desire to feel or look sexy.

'They were really very articulate about those decisions being very consciously made,' said Dr Rebekah Willett, lecturer in education at London University's Institute of Education and one of the authors of the report.

A padded bra, for example, was often preferred by girls not because of its sexual connotations, but because they found it more comfortable, or because it was 'less revealing because everyone kind of had a very similar shape', she explained.

Concerns remain, nevertheless, and the issue goes far beyond a supply and demand equation in the retail market. Glossy advertisements on billboards and in the media, as well as music videos on channels like MTV, where viewers are mostly in their teens and twenties, are increasingly becoming more revealing and provocative as they strive to stand out.

In April, the broadcasting watchdog Ofcom ruled that a racy performance by pop star Christina Aguilera and her backing dancers on last year's final of *The X Factor*, broadcast before the 9pm 'watershed', had been 'at the very margin of acceptability'. The routine had sparked 2,868 complaints to the media regulator.

The role models presented online, in magazines and on television have had an impact on the way young people, especially girls, see themselves, experts believe. Tanith Carey, journalist and author of *Where Has My Little Girl Gone?*, said girls were caught up in a 'perfect storm', constantly being bombarded by media influences.

'Girls feel at a younger age than ever that they can't live up to these stereotypes. That's when they get feelings of worthlessness or depression,' she told TESS. The need 'to attract attention or achieve validation through looking sexy and wearing provocative clothes' was tied to a lack of self-esteem, she suggested.

Linda Thompson, a development officer funded by the Scottish Government and based at the Women's Support Network in Glasgow, specialises in talks and workshops for young people, parents and teachers, on sexualisation and objectification issues. She agrees that girls' self-perception and the pressure on them to adhere to stereotypes can lead to risky behaviour.

'Our hyper-sexualised culture has created an environment in which young people are almost expected to brand themselves in a highly sexualised way in order to gain value and popularity,' she said.

Girls started to believe that to dress and behave in a certain way, and to agree to engage in sexual behaviour, such as sexting – texting explicit messages or pictures – was a way to become popular, she said. Some as young as 14 had spoken to her about having to 'build their brand', she added.

The choice, in many cases, was 'to be invisible, or to be highly sexual. At that age, forming your identity, forming your ideas of peer group norms, it is very difficult for a girl to say: "I will be invisible, I will be the prude',"' Ms Thompson said.

Pressure to adhere to stereotypes does not just affect girls. Boys often felt under pressure to behave in a certain way too, said Ms Thompson. 'I think young men are being backed into very clear, tight gender rules,' she said. 'It is expected that part of masculinity is to be predatory.'

Boys, therefore, were more inclined to ask girls for explicit pictures, with some collecting large numbers of pictures on their phones and on USB memory sticks, and even sharing and swapping pictures with their peers.

This has been enabled and supported by the emergence of social networking sites and constant accessibility of the Internet, which has made it more difficult for adults to control the content to which children are exposed.

According to figures published by Ofcom in July, 79 per cent of children in Scotland have access to the Internet at home through a PC or laptop, and only in a quarter of those cases were parental controls in place to limit their access to inappropriate content.

Scottish youngsters with home Internet access spend an average of 11.4 hours per week online, the statistics revealed, although they did not include the 54 per cent of youngsters who are able to access the Internet instantly from their smart phones (EU Kids Online).

Permanent Internet access, combined with peer pressure and natural curiosity among young people, has also led to another concern for adults: children and young people's exposure to pornography.

The EU Kids Online study showed earlier this year that a quarter of children in the UK aged nine to 16 had seen sexual images in the past 12 months, and 46 per cent of these had seen them online.

Six per cent of children aged 11-16 exposed to sexual images had seen pictures or video of someone having sex online, the research revealed, and one in 50 had seen images,

video or a movie that 'showed sex in a violent way'.

'Young men I have talked to have spoken about the pressure to say that they love pornography and carry it around with them, to have their stock of images on their phone,' Ms Thompson told TESS. 'Young men will say "I have to have my porn, because if I don't, people will call me gay".'

Free sites were especially popular with young people. 'The supposedly amateur, user-uploaded pornography will be really popular with young people because it is free,' Ms Thompson said, adding that often the content was 'more extreme stuff' in terms of the levels of physical extremity and violence in it.

'Young people don't necessarily see the violence there; they don't look at it with an understanding that that is a human being that is happening to,' she said.

But young people did not only encounter sexual content by choice. Often, they stumbled upon it accidentally, or were shown it by peers, she pointed out.

'I did work recently with a group of young women and they talked about how uncomfortable they are in the school setting, sitting in the classroom, with young men sitting at the back of a class watching porn on their mobile phones. They know this happens, but they can't challenge it, because if they do, they get labelled as a prude.'

Sue Palmer, former headteacher and author of *Toxic Childhood*, said she was especially concerned about the impact of pornography on young people's perception of relationships. Exposure to online content such as 'gonzo porn', which gives the illusion that it is being filmed by participants, failed to highlight the intimacy essential to healthy relationships, she said.

Ms Palmer called on the teaching profession to put its voice behind policy proposals such as UK Communications Minister Ed Vaizey's suggestion that a new communications bill might legislate for a mandatory Internet filter so adults would have to 'opt in' if they wished to access adult content from their computers or phones. Currently, parents and teachers have to put in place filters and protection to opt out of such content.

Recommendations from the Bailey Review, accepted by the Westminster Government, include a wide range of measures: a covering-up of sexualised images on the front pages of newspapers and magazines; measures to make it easier for parents to block adult and age-restricted material from the Internet by giving them a choice at the point of purchase on whether they want adult content access; and guidelines for retailers on the design, display and marketing of clothes and products for children.

Mr Bailey told TESS that people working in education also had a role to play. While there was a primary responsibility on parents, educators also had responsibilities – firstly to help build children's emotional resilience by giving them the confidence to navigate the digital landscape in particular; and secondly to find ways of engaging parents in the debate.

The latter was much harder, he said. 'Some parents will engage willingly, so you might find a discussion and awareness event oversubscribed, while others at a different school will not want to engage at all. I'm keen that we find better ways of engaging with parents to help them help their children.'

The NSPCC, in its submission to the Bailey Review, also stressed the importance of building resilience in children to a sexualised environment. Jon Brown, head of strategy and development (sexual abuse), said: 'We feel, and young people tell us this, that sex education is really important and we are told that it does not happen early enough.'

Teachers often did not feel confident enough to discuss topics relating to sex with children and young people, and the NSPCC would like to see 'at least some consideration given to special training for PSE teachers', he added. This would ensure each school had some staff confident in teaching the subject.

Girls told the charity they felt they would be able to talk more openly if PSE was taught on a single gender basis, Mr Brown said. The training of peer mentors was another measure the NSPCC would welcome, as most young people turned to their peers first for information about sex.

Ms Thompson urged teachers to make room across the curriculum to discuss sexualisation in a range of subjects, which could include biology, health and well-being and religious and moral education.

Tanith Carey, however, believes the role of schools in tackling the sexualisation of young people should go beyond curriculum subjects. Headteachers should help parents to become more aware of the problem, if necessary with the help of outside organisations and speakers, she said.

Heads also needed to consider seriously the appropriateness of events such as proms for primary school children and beauty tents at school fetes, and try to 'set a standard and draw a line in the sand', she said.

The focus in school should not simply be on children's academic achievements, but giving young people, especially girls, self-esteem and belief in their own talents from an early age.

'A lot of it is about giving children capability, allowing them to achieve a sense of personal power, questioning the influences, about valuing our girls in a particular way,' Ms Carey said. She urged teachers to be more aware of how their actions made children feel. 'We have to remember that how we speak is how they think we feel about them,' she said.

5 August 2011

⇨ The above information is reprinted with kind permission from TES. Please visit www.tes.co.uk for further information.

Letting children be children

Report of an independent review of the commercialisation and sexualisation of childhood by Reg Bailey.

Theme 1 – the 'wallpaper' of children's lives

Overview

⇨ We are all living in an increasingly sexual and sexualised culture, although it is far from clear how we arrived at this point.

⇨ Many parents feel that this culture is often inappropriate for their children and they want more power to say 'no'.

⇨ Some parts of the business world and sections of the media seem to have lost their connection to parents and this is compounded in some new media where there is limited regulation.

⇨ Where regulation does exist, regulators need to connect better with parents and encourage businesses to comply with the 'spirit of the regulation'. Where regulation does not exist, businesses need to behave more responsibly.

What we would like to see

That sexualised images used in public places and on television, the Internet, music videos, magazines, newspapers and other places are more in line with what parents find acceptable, and that public space becomes more family-friendly.

Recommendations

1. Ensuring that magazines and newspapers with sexualised images on their covers are not in easy sight of children. Retail associations in the news industry should do more to encourage observance of the voluntary code of practice on the display of magazines and newspapers with sexualised images on their covers. Publishers and distributors should provide such magazines in modesty sleeves, or make modesty boards available, to all outlets they supply and strongly encourage the appropriate display of their publications. Retailers should be open and transparent to show that they welcome and will act on customer feedback regarding magazine displays.

2. Reducing the amount of on-street advertising containing sexualised imagery in locations where children are likely to see it. The advertising industry should take into account the social responsibility clause of the Committee of Advertising Practice (CAP) code when considering placement of advertisements with sexualised imagery near schools, in the same way as they already do for alcohol advertisements. The Advertising Standards Authority (ASA) should place stronger emphasis on the location of an advertisement, and the number of children likely to be exposed to it, when considering whether an on-street advertisement is compliant with the CAP code. The testing of standards that the ASA undertakes with parents (see Recommendation 7) should also cover parental views on location of advertising in public spaces.

3. Ensuring the content of pre-watershed television programming better meets parents' expectations. There are concerns among parents about the content of certain programmes shown before the watershed. The watershed was introduced to protect children, and pre-watershed programming should therefore be developed and regulated with a greater weight towards the attitudes and views of parents, rather than 'viewers' as a whole. In addition, broadcasters should involve parents on an ongoing basis in testing the standards by which family viewing on television is assessed and the Office of Communications (Ofcom) should extend its existing research into the views of parents on the watershed. Broadcasters and Ofcom should report annually on how they have specifically engaged parents over the previous year, what they have learnt and what they are doing differently as a result.

4. Introducing Age Rating for Music Videos. Government should consult as a matter of priority on whether music videos should continue to be treated differently from other genres, and whether the exemption from the Video Recordings Act 1984 and 2010, which allows them to be sold without a rating or certificate, should be removed. As well as ensuring hard copy sales are only made on an age-appropriate basis, removal of the exemption would assist broadcasters and Internet companies in ensuring that the content is made available responsibly.

5. Making it easier for parents to block adult and age-restricted material from the Internet. To provide a consistent level of protection across all media, as a matter of urgency, the Internet industry should ensure that customers must make an active choice over what sort of content they want to allow their children to access. To facilitate this, the Internet industry must act decisively to develop and introduce effective parental controls, with government regulation if voluntary action is not forthcoming within a reasonable timescale. In addition, those providing content which is age-restricted, whether by law or company policy, should seek robust means of age verification as well as making it easy for parents to block underage access.

Theme 2 – clothing, products and services for children

Overview

⇨ Sexualised and gender-stereotyped clothing, products and services for children are the biggest areas of concern for parents and many non-commercial organisations contributing to the review, with interest fanned by a sometimes prurient press.

⇨ The issues are rarely clear-cut, with a fine balance on a number of points – taste, preference, choice, affordability, fashion and gender preferences.

⇨ Retailers are aware of the issues and sensitivities and are responding. They need to be explicitly and systematically family friendly, from design and buying through to display and marketing.

What we would like to see

That retailers do not sell or market inappropriate clothing, products or services for children.

Recommendation

6. Developing a retail code of good practice on retailing to children. Retailers, alongside their trade associations, should develop and comply with a voluntary code of good practice for all aspects of retailing to children. The British Retail Consortium (BRC) should continue its work in this area as a matter of urgency and encourage non-BRC members to sign up to its code.

Theme 3 – children as consumers

Overview

⇨ We all live in a commercial world and children are under pressure from a range of sources to act as consumers.

⇨ We do not want to cut children off from the commercial world completely as we believe that it brings benefits and parents tell us that they want to manage the issue themselves, supported by proportionate regulation and responsible businesses.

⇨ While adults may understand that companies might look to 'push the boundaries' when advertising to them, children are especially vulnerable and need to be given special consideration. Special measures already exist in advertising and marketing regulations to protect children but some gaps exist.

⇨ Regulators cannot realistically be expected to anticipate detailed developments in the new media. However, an absence of regulation does not absolve businesses from acting responsibly by themselves.

What we would like to see

That the regulations protecting children from excessive commercial pressures are comprehensive and effective across all media and in line with parental expectations.

That marketers do not exploit any gaps in advertising regulation in order to unduly influence the choices children make as consumers.

That parents and children have a sound awareness and understanding of marketing techniques and regulation.

Recommendations

7. Ensuring that the regulation of advertising reflects more closely parents' and children's views. The Advertising Standards Authority (ASA) should conduct research with parents and children on a regular basis in order to gauge their views on the ASA's approach to regulation and on the ASA's decisions, publishing the results and subsequent action taken in their annual report.

8. Prohibiting the employment of children as brand ambassadors and in peer-to-peer marketing. The Committee of Advertising Practice and other advertising and marketing bodies should urgently explore whether, as many parents believe, the advertising self-regulatory codes should prohibit the employment of children under the age of 16 as brand ambassadors or in peer-to-peer marketing – where people are paid, or paid in kind, to promote products, brands or services.

9. Defining a child as under the age of 16 in all types of advertising regulation. The ASA should conduct research with parents, children and young people to determine whether the ASA should always define a child as a person under the age of 16, in line with the Committee of Advertising Practice and Broadcast Committee of Advertising Practice codes.

10. Raising parental awareness of marketing and advertising techniques. Industry and regulators should work together to improve parental awareness of marketing

and advertising techniques and of advertising regulation and complaints processes and to promote industry best practice.

11. Quality assurance for media and commercial literacy resources and education for children. These resources should always include education to help children develop their emotional resilience to the commercial and sexual pressures that today's world places on them. Providers should commission independent evaluation of their provision, not solely measuring take-up but, crucially, to assess its effectiveness. Those bodies with responsibilities for promoting media literacy, including Ofcom and the BBC, should encourage the development of minimum standards guidance for the content of media and commercial literacy education and resources to children.

Theme 4 – Making parents' voices heard

Overview

⇨ Parents have told us that they feel they cannot make their voices heard, and that they often lack the confidence to speak out on sexualisation and commercialisation issues for fear of being labelled a prude or out of touch.

⇨ Business and industry sectors and their regulators need to make clear that they welcome, and take seriously, feedback on these subjects.

⇨ Given the technology available, regulators and businesses should be able to find more effective ways to encourage parents to tell them what they think, quickly and easily, and to be transparent in telling parents how they are responding to that feedback.

⇨ Once parents know that their views are being taken seriously, we would expect them to respond positively towards companies that listen to their concerns.

What we would like to see

That parents find it easier to voice their concerns, are listened to more readily when they do, and have their concerns visibly acted on by businesses and regulators.

Recommendations

12. Ensuring greater transparency in the regulatory framework by creating a single website for regulators. There is a variety of co-, self- and statutory regulators across the media, communications and retail industries. Regulators should work together to create a single website to act as an interface between themselves and parents. This will set out simply and clearly what parents can do if they feel a programme, advertisement, product or service is inappropriate for their children; explain the legislation in simple terms; and provide links to quick and easy complaints forms on regulators' own individual websites. This single website could also provide a way for parents to provide informal feedback and comments, with an option to do so anonymously, which regulators can use as an extra gauge of parental views. Results of regulators' decisions, and their reactions to any informal feedback, should be published regularly on the single site.

13. Making it easier for parents to express their views to businesses about goods and services. All businesses that market goods or services to children should have a one-click link to their complaints service from their home page, clearly labelled 'complaints'. Information provided as part of the complaints and feedback process should state explicitly that the business welcomes comments and complaints from parents about issues affecting children. Businesses should also provide timely feedback to customers in reaction to customer comment. For retail businesses this should form part of their code of good practice (see Theme 2, Recommendation 6), and should also cover how to make it easier and more parent-friendly for complaints to be made in store.

Conclusion

Overview

⇨ The Government should monitor implementation and formally review progress in 18 months' time.

⇨ A stocktake, to include an independent assessment of progress, should report on the success or otherwise of business, regulators and government in adopting the recommendations of this review.

⇨ If the stocktake reaches the conclusion that insufficient progress has been made, our view is that the Government would be fully entitled to bring forward appropriate statutory measures to ensure action is taken.

What we want to see

That the actions recommended in the review are implemented by broadcasters, advertisers, retailers, other businesses and regulators within a reasonable timescale.

Recommendation

14. Ensuring that businesses and others take action on these recommendations. Government should take stock of progress against the recommendations of this review in 18 months' time. This stocktake should report on the success or otherwise of businesses and others in adopting these recommendations. If it concludes that insufficient progress has been made, the Government should consider taking the most effective action available, including regulating through legislation if necessary, to achieve the recommended outcome.

June 2011

⇨ The above information is an extract from the report *Letting Children be Children* and is reprinted with kind permission from the Department for Education. Please visit www.education.gov.uk for further information.

Let Girls Be Girls campaign

Let Girls Be Girls was launched in early 2010, and grew from Mumsnetters' concern that an increasingly sexualised culture was dripping, toxically, into the lives of children.

The campaign aims to curb the premature sexualisation of children by asking retailers to commit not to sell products which play upon, emphasise or exploit their sexuality. Earlier this year, the campaign was extended to tackle lads' mags, calling on newsagents and supermarkets not to display them in children's sight.

We're very pleased that the key 'asks' of our Let Girls Be Girls and Lads' Mags campaign have been endorsed by the Government's Bailey Review into the sexualisation and commercialisation of childhood. The report proposes tighter controls on sexualised products aimed at children, and calls for magazines which feature sexualised imagery not to be displayed where children can easily see them. It shows just what can be achieved when we get together to change things that seem, on the surface, to be 'just the way things are'.

'Little girls are being groomed into passively accepting their place as objects in our increasingly pornified culture, and it stinks'

TenaciousG

More about the Bailey Review

The review makes further recommendations about the exposure of children to sexualised imagery. It proposes that explicit ads, music videos and TV programmes – described as a 'wallpaper of sexual images that surround children' – should be subject to tighter control, with age-ratings on music videos, and stricter enforcement of the television watershed.

It recommends that outdoor advertising featuring sexual imagery should not be displayed in areas near schools or playgrounds, and that parents should have a one-stop portal to enable them to complain about products, ads or services more easily.

The review also proposes that Internet users should have to make 'an active choice over whether they allow adult content or not'.

Why Let Girls Be Girls?

It's no secret that the worlds of entertainment and celebrity encourage girls to believe their sexual attractiveness is paramount – and many Mumsnetters were alarmed that this trend was becoming increasingly visible in products marketed at young children.

They felt that a growing number of toys, clothes ('sexy' slogans on young girls' clothing, high heels for five-year-olds) and accessories (Playboy-branded stationery sets? Good grief) seemed designed to encourage children to enter the world of adult sexuality when they should still be – well, children.

Like many others, we're worried about the long-term impact of this trend.

You don't have to be a feminist to believe that little girls shouldn't be told that a vital quality to cultivate is that of being attractive to boys. Nor do you have to be Mary Whitehouse to believe that it's not great for girls – or boys – to grow up thinking that being feminine is all about a pornography-inspired pastiche of female sexuality. The trend towards premature sexualisation:

⇨ introduces children to the world of adult sexuality, when elsewhere we are rightly encouraging them to resist the pressure to become sexually active at a young age

⇨ tells girls in particular that the most important quality they need is 'sexiness', and not cleverness, sportiness, application or ambition

⇨ tells girls and boys that female sexuality is all about pleasing others

⇨ encourages a culture in which children are viewed as sexually available.

'Kids should be allowed to be kids, not be forced into mini adulthood when they're far too young physically and emotionally'

Fords

Moral panic?

This aim of this campaign is not to police the developing sexuality of children, or to deny that such a thing exists. Mumsnetters, on the whole, aren't interested in protecting a misty ideal of 'childhood innocence' – in fact, they're pretty keen on being as honest as possible about sex.

But many argue that it's difficult for children to learn about sexuality – and to decide for themselves how they'd like to express it – when they are bombarded with an all-pervasive 'commodified' version of female sexuality. This campaign aims, not to remove children's control over their sexuality, but to give it back.

And clearly, sexualisation doesn't only affect children: many Mumsnetters feel that women too are, to varying degrees, affected by the sexual culture we live in. What can be done? The truth is, we don't know. But we thought that our collective 'consumer heft' could be a good place to start, so we worked to influence the products that were being sold to our daughters, in the hope that the next generation of women will be better able to choose who they want to be.

Which retailers have backed the campaign?

Major retailers who have signed up include Bhs, Sainsburys, Primark, Matalan, George at Asda, Tesco, Next, Boots, Clarks, Debenhams, John Lewis, Marks & Spencer, Boden, Sweetling Bras and Mothercare.

Why retailers?

Of course, the premature sexualisation of children is not driven only by retail and marketing. Music, TV, pop promos, newspapers and lads' mags are all in the dock – but turning back the tide of pop culture felt like a big ask, even for Mumsnetters.

We did think, though, that we could let retailers know how we felt about this development – so, in February 2010, we wrote to them, asking them to do their bit to help reverse this trend.

We were absolutely delighted that so many high-street names agreed to take the lead on this very important issue. Plenty of retailers, including Boden, Startright, House of Fraser, Mothercare and Asda signed up to Let Girls Be Girls almost immediately, and other big names – John Lewis, Tesco, M&S, Bhs, Boots, Zara, and Next among others – followed close behind.

Now, as the government publishes it's Review of the Sexualisation and Commercialisation of Children, the British Retailers Consortium has launched a new set of stricter 'best practice' guidelines to ensure that responsible retailers meet parents' concerns.

What we asked retailers to do

Those retailers who have signed up to Let Girls Be Girls have agreed 'not to sell products which exploit, emphasise or play upon "children's sexuality".'

We mentioned a few examples of inappropriate products in our letter to retailers – children's underwear which mimics adult lingerie, 'grown up' heels for little girls, 'sexy' or provocative slogans on clothing – but we deliberately didn't provide a definitive list of inappropriate products. We want to encourage retailers to become self-policing, and we feel they're more likely to do so without a list to 'tick'. We're also wary of appearing tacitly to endorse an item, simply because it's not yet been drawn to our attention.

However, this is a learning process for all of us; it's possible that some retailers might slip up – so please do let us know if you see products which concern you. In this situation, we'll first ask Mumsnetters what they think, and if there is a broad consensus that the product in question does sexualise children, we will raise the issue with the retailer concerned, and work with them to resolve the problem. If an acceptable solution can't ultimately be found, the retailer's accreditation could be removed.

Let Girls Be Girls is a rolling campaign: new products are hitting the shops all the time, and there are still plenty of retailers who haven't yet signed up.

What about parental responsibility?

Of course we're not suggesting that retailers should shoulder all the responsibility for turning back the tide. We understand that parents have the option of not buying products which sexualise children, and that a small minority of parents might actively wish to dress their eight-year-olds like mini-adults, teetering in heels and a provocatively-sloganed top.

But we believe few parents make an active choice to do so – we know from experience that most parents are low on energy, and struggle to resist 'pester power' at the best of times. Holding the line against a furious nine-year-old can sometimes seem like a battle not worth fighting, and the more widely available these products are, the more acceptable – even inevitable- – they are perceived to be.

But working together, we think we can make a difference – and ultimately, we believe that the retailers who have signed up to the campaign will benefit from the support of the vast majority of parents who want products which 'Let Girls Be Girls'.

The effects of premature sexualisation on girls

Authorities as varied as the NSPCC, the NUT and the Archbishop of Canterbury are concerned that this generation is being sexualised before they reach their teens, with, according to the experts, disastrous implications for their self-worth.

⇨ In 2007, a study by the American Psychological Association found that: 'Sexualisation has negative effects in a variety of domains, including physical and mental health, and healthy sexual development.' Possible ongoing effects identified by the research include: low self-esteem, poor academic performance, depression, and eating disorders such as anorexia.

⇨ A 2008 study by Girlguiding UK and the Mental Health Foundation found that premature sexualisation and pressure to grow up too quickly are two 'key influences' in the anxiety felt by girls.

According to Dr Andrew McCulloch, Chief Executive of the Mental Health Foundation, 'Girls and young women are being forced to grow up at an unnatural pace in a society that we, as adults, have created and it's damaging their emotional well-being. We are creating a generation under stress.'

⇨ Information from Mumsnet. For further information please visit www.mumsnet.com.

Review into sexualisation of young people published

An independent review into the sexualisation of young people, conducted by psychologist Dr Linda Papadopoulos, was welcomed by Home Secretary Alan Johnson today.

Commissioned by the Home Office, the review forms part of the Government's strategy to tackle Violence Against Women and Girls (VAWG) and looks at how sexualised images and messages may be affecting the development of children and young people and influencing cultural norms. It also examines the evidence for a link between sexualisation and violence.

Key recommendations include:

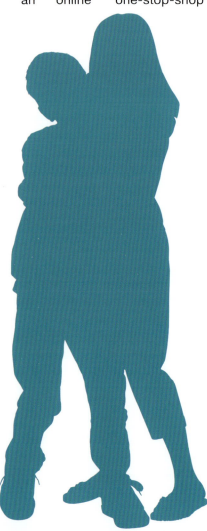

⇨ the Government to launch an online 'one-stop-shop' to allow the public to voice their concerns regarding irresponsible marketing which sexualises children, with an onus on regulatory authorities to take action. The website could help inform future government policy by giving parents a forum to raise issues of concern regarding the sexualisation of young people

⇨ the Government should support the Advertising Standards Agency (ASA) to take steps to extend the existing regulatory standards to include commercial websites

⇨ broadcasters are required to ensure that music videos featuring sexual posing or sexually suggestive lyrics are broadcast only after the 'watershed'

⇨ the Government to support the NSPCC in its work with manufacturers and retailers to encourage corporate responsibility with regard to sexualised merchandise. Guidelines should be issued for retailers following consultation with major clothing retailers and parents' groups

⇨ games consoles should be sold with parental controls already switched on. Purchasers can choose to 'unlock' the console if they wish to allow access to adult and online content.

Dr Papadopoulos has worked closely with the Home Office in developing the current national awareness campaign targeting violence within teenagers' relationships. A pack for teachers and pupils to accompany the campaign will shortly be made available to all schools. The Government is also committed to introducing the subject of violence against women and girls and gender equality into the national curriculum, both of which are recommendations outlined in this review. The full list of recommendations will now be considered in more detail.

Statement from the Home Secretary

Alan Johnson said, 'We know that parents are concerned about the pressures their children are under at a much younger age, which is why we have already committed to a number of the recommendations in this report.

'Changing attitudes will take time but it is essential if we are going to stop the sexualisation which contributes to violence against women and girls.

'I would like to thank Dr Linda Papadopoulos for producing this review, with recommendations which will contribute to the ongoing debate around this complex issue.

'We will now consider the full list of recommendations in more detail and continue to ensure that young people's development and well-being are a top priority.'

Statement from psychologist Dr Linda Papadopoulos

Dr Papadopoulos said, 'As a psychologist and as a parent, I welcomed the opportunity to take a critical look at the sexualisation of young people.

'Over the past few months I have spoken to many people including young people, parents, teachers and professionals and it is clear to me that this is a very emotive issue.

'I wanted to ensure that this was not an opinion piece, but a review based on real data and academic research which will help generate further debate and inform decisions about how to address these issues going forward.'

Statement from the Children's Minister

Delyth Morgan said, 'Children today are growing up in a complex and changing world and they need to learn how to stay safe and resist inappropriate pressures. That is why we are making Personal, Social, Health and Economic (PSHE) education statutory so that we can teach children about the real life issues they will face as they grow up.

'PSHE already includes teaching about advertising and body image and from 2011 will include issues around violence against women and girls. The PSHE curriculum is age appropriate to give children and young people the right information at the right time to help them make the best choices and to develop their confidence.

'We are supporting schools with new guidance to help raise awareness among teachers about violence against women and girls, so that they can prevent and respond to these issues, and to show them how to address it in the curriculum.

'We have also recently launched a new campaign Click Clever Click Safe to help children and young people understand some of the risks they are exposed to when they go online. This will give parents the confidence to help their children enjoy the Internet safely.'

26 February 2010

⇨ The above information is reprinted with kind permission from the PSHE Association. Please visit www.pshe-association.org.uk for further information.

© *PSHE Association*

The Home Office report on child sexualisation is a 100-page *Cosmopolitan* article

***Article originally appeared in* The Telegraph.**

By Toby Young

Today's Home Office report on the sexualisation of children feels like a bit of cheap electioneering rather than a serious piece of research. The report, by Dr Linda Papadopoulos, claims to have established that there's a 'clear link' between sexual imagery and violence against women and makes a number of proposals, including selling mobile phones and games consoles with parental controls switched on, stopping the sale of lad mags to under-16s and banning sexualised imagery in adverts.

The report doesn't make the case for these proposals on moral grounds, but for reasons of public safety and, in particular, the safety of women. Here's the key passage:

The evidence gathered in the review suggests a clear link between consumption of sexualised images, tendency to view women as objects and the acceptance of aggressive attitudes and behaviour as the norm.

Both the images we consume and the way we consume them are lending credence to the idea that women are there to be used and that men are there to use them.

We've heard about this 'clear link' before and it would be quite something if Dr Linda Papadopoulos has managed to establish it since no one else has. Suppose a 'clear link' did exist between sexual imagery and violence towards women. You'd expect the latter to have increased in direct proportion to the prevalence of former, right? And no one would dispute that sexual imagery is more prevalent now than it was in, say, 1997, not least because access to the Internet has increased exponentially since then.

But according to Harriet Harman, the Minister for Women, incidents of domestic violence fell 64 per cent between 1997 and 2009. These figures aren't just for reported crimes, either. They come from the British Crime Survey, which includes crimes not reported to the police. According to the British Crime Survey for 2008/09, the number of domestic violence incidents has more than halved.

Now I'm not suggesting for a moment that the current levels of domestic violence are acceptable. In 2008/09, domestic violence accounted for nearly one in three (31 per cent) incidents of violence against women, equivalent to approximately 226,000 separate acts. That is an appalling statistic and, clearly, a problem we ought to be tackling. All I'm saying is that there is absolutely no proof that there is a link between domestic violence and the prevalence of sexual imagery.

What about rape? Admittedly, that has increased. According to the British Crime Survey for 2007/08, there were 6,281 recorded instances of 'Rape of a female' in 1997, compared to 11,648 in 2007/08. However, this jump is largely explained by the replacement of the Sexual Offences Act 1956 by the Sexual Offences Act 2003, which broadened the definition of 'rape' to include penetration of the mouth. I'm not saying that 'rape' shouldn't have been redefined in this way, only that it is this redefinition that accounts for the increase between 1997 and 2007/08. And, incidentally, between 2006/07 and 2007/08 the number of rapes of women declined by eight per cent.

Nevertheless, according to Dr Linda Papadopoulos there is a 'clear link'. So who is this brilliant social scientist who has made this discovery?

According to the preamble to the Home Office report, she 'is one of the most well-known and respect psychologists working in the UK'. I can't argue with the 'well-known' part because Dr Papadopoulos is the resident psychologist on *Big Brother*, the Channel 4 reality show. Indeed, she is so 'respected' by the producers of reality shows that she also appeared on *Celebrity Fit Club* and *My Big Breasts and Me*. In case you're not convinced by these 'credentials', let's not forget that she has also appeared on *Celebrity Mastermind* (special subject: the band Nirvana).

'This report is a not a serious investigation ... it posits a link between ... violence and various things that Dr Papadopoulus disapproves of – such as lad mags and airbrushed photographs'

So what proof does Dr Papadopoulos offer of this 'clear link'? I've drilled down into her Home Office report and, in fact, it offers no proof whatsoever. For instance, here's a passage from Chapter Six ('The Impact of Sexualisation'):

The sexualisation of women – and, more widely, the pornification of culture – can put pressure on boys to act out a version of masculinity based on the display of power over women. ... [snip] ... Given this, it is perhaps not too much of a leap to posit a link between the messages being sent out to boys and the normalisation of aggressive – or even violent behaviour – towards girls and women ...

Here's another passage from the introduction to Chapter Seven ('Sexualisation and Violence'):

Sexual abuse and sexual violence are, thankfully, at the extreme end of the spectrum of impacts of sexualisation. Nevertheless, it is imperative that we acknowledge the very real possibility that, say, pornography that shows girls talking with relish about pre-teen sexual exploits, or highly realistic video games where players take on the role of stalker and rapist might start to blur the boundaries between what is acceptable and what is not.

The sexualisation of women can put pressure on boys ... it is perhaps not too much of a leap to posit ... the very real possibility that ...

This isn't the language of a social scientist, but of a journalist — and a fairly sloppy one at that. It's pure conjecture. It's the sort of thing you'd expect to find in Cosmopolitan — which isn't surprising since Dr Papadopoulos writes for Cosmopolitan. She's entitled to her opinion, of course, but that's all it is — opinion. There's no factual evidence in the report that sexual imagery causes violence against women.

On the basis of what is, in effect, a 100-page Cosmopolitan article, Dr Papadopoulus makes 32 recommendations, including banning job centres from advertising jobs in lapdancing clubs, forcing magazines to indicate where photographs have been air-brushed and outlawing inappropriate music videos before the 9pm watershed. The most pernicious of these proposals involve changes to the national curriculum. For instance, it is proposed that Personal, Social, Health and Economic education, Sex and Relationships education and Digital Literacy education are all made compulsory. Please, God, no.

The most revealing recommendation made by Dr Papadopoulos is the following:

Funding be made available for research that will strengthen the evidence base. There is a particular need for longitudinal research; research into the impact of sexualisation on black and minority ethnic groups, gay and lesbian groups and disabled populations; and carefully designed ethical research into the impact on child populations.

In other words, let's commission some research to demonstrate the 'clear link' that I have palpably failed to demonstrate in this 100-page document.

This report is not a serious investigation into the causes of violence against women. Rather, it posits a link between that violence and various things that Dr Papadopoulus disapproves of – such as lad mags and airbrushed photographs – in a spurious attempt to either ban them or regulate them on grounds of public safety.

I'm not suggesting that violence against women isn't a serious problem. But there is no evidence that the measures proposed in this report will have any impact on it – zilch, nada, bupkis. It's a vote grabber and not a serious attempt to tackle the issue.

26 February 2010

⇨ The above article originally appeared in The Telegraph Please visit www.telegraph.co.uk.

Sexualised wallpaper

An extract from Not in front of the children. Sexualisation: Impacts and Interventions.

By Kate Marvin

The main basis for concern regarding sexualisation of children and young people is the idea that we are living in a world which is saturated with sexual images and messages and that these messages may have a detrimental effect on children and young people. Here some of the evidence around these concerns will be examined.

A survey by the Girl Guiding Association and Child Wise (2011) asked girls aged seven to 21 how they felt about a number of issues including those to do with media and pressure to conform. The survey found that 55% of the young women involved felt that 'Pressure to look like a celebrity' was one of the main causes of stress among girls their age. The same survey also reported that only 23% of girls felt that girls and young women were portrayed fairly in the media and 90% thought that TV and magazines focus too much on what women look like, instead of what they achieve. The majority of participants in this survey also reported feeling under pressure, with 82% reporting that there was a lot of pressure on girls to wear the latest fashions and have the latest gadgets. These results show that girls and young women are aware of the messages given by the mass media. While young women are reporting being affected and feeling pressure from these messages, these results also suggest that young women have an awareness that what they see, hear and read does not necessarily reflect reality.

There is some evidence presented in the academic literature concerning the effects of particular elements of the mass media, which collectively allow a more holistic picture of the issues under discussion to be created.

A study by Goodin et al. (2011) conducted a content analysis of American children's clothing websites designed to assess the prevalence of sexualising characteristics. The clothes included were made for children approximately seven to 14 years old and were considered to have sexualising characteristics if they (a) revealed a sexualised body part, (b) emphasised a sexualised body part, (c) had characteristics associated with sexiness and/or (d) displayed writing with sexualised content. The results showed that 29.4% of the clothing examined displayed sexual characteristics based on these criteria and that of the clothing with sexual characteristics 86.4% also displayed 'child-like' characteristics. The authors argue that this could serve to blur the boundaries between what is appropriate for children's and adult's clothing and may contribute to children's sexualisation and self-objectification.

An Australian study by Fabrianesi et al. (2008) also conducted a content analysis; however, the focus here was on the representation of celebrities in magazines aimed at pre-adolescent and teenage girls. The study considered the number of images of celebrities as well as the context in which they were shown and the primary career of the individuals. Unsurprisingly the vast majority of featured celebrities in both pre-adolescent and teenage magazines were actors, singers or socialites, with very few images of women in other professions such as sports-women making an appearance. What may be more surprising is that there was very little difference in the celebrity content of magazines aimed at five to 12 year olds and those targeted at a 14-17-year old market, with eight of the 12 most featured individuals in teenage magazines also being in the top 12 celebrities featured in content aimed at younger girls. This research also found that of the twelve most commonly featured celebrities in pre-adolescent magazines at least five had been publicly recorded as suffering from some form of disordered eating, three had been recorded as suffering from drug and alcohol abuse and one had participated in a pornographic film which was readily available over the Internet. The researchers in this study argue that this type of content analysis provides evidence that the role models provided for children and young people may not be realistic or age appropriate and that they encourage young people to internalise strict beauty ideals from a very young age.

The content of television programmes aimed at young people has also been separately evaluated. Eyal et al. (2011) conducted an analysis of the sexual messages presented by the twenty television programs most popular among teenagers both in 2001-02 and 2004-05. Sexual messages included talk about sex, sexual behaviour and sexual intercourse. The study looked at the frequency and context of sexual messages as well as the presence of safer sex messages and portrayals of the consequences of sexual intercourse. The study found that 83% of programmes contained at least one scene with sexual content in the 2001-02 sample, which dropped to 70% in the 2004-05 sample; the average number of scenes remained constant at 6.7 scenes per hour. On average only approximately 10% of programmes which included sexual content also contained messages around sexual risk taking and safer sex. There was a rise in the number of programmes showing negative consequences of sexual intercourse between 2001-01 and 2004-05, however, the number of programmes discussing any consequences of sexual intercourse were small and so results should be viewed with caution. The results of this study suggest that the sexual content of television programmes aimed at young people is relatively high and that discussion around risks and safety is somewhat sparse.

All of these content analysis studies give an idea of the types of media and products that young people are exposed to and suggest that there are a high volume of sexual messages being given to young people on a daily basis. What this information does not tell us is how young people may be interpreting and processing the information they receive or if the presence of sexualised media in itself has any particular effect.

March 2012

⇨ Information from NHS Sheffield. www.sexualhealthsheffield.nhs.uk

All of our concern: commercialisation, sexualisation and hypermasculinity

Extract from a report by Family Lives.

Executive summary

All of our concern

Family Lives has published this report to take forward the useful debate that has been most recently built upon by the 2011 Review of the Commercialisation and Sexualisation of Childhood undertaken by Reg Bailey. This report seeks to address issues that the Bailey Review gave less time to and makes recommendations to take the agenda forward in a way which empowers young people and their parents.

This report will discuss the progress made since the Bailey Review and identify areas which still require policy makers' and parents' attention.

⇨ Family Lives believes that much of the commercialisation and sexualisation debate has been framed around girls and neglects to consider how boys have been affected by these pressures and how to engage them in preventative strategies. This report will address this gap.

⇨ This report will also examine a serious, yet neglected topic: peer–on-peer sexual exploitation and violence. The report examines the consequences of extreme gender identification, specifically hypermasculinity, which is associated with sexual violence against girls. Tackling this problem is essential to ensuring that all individuals are free from sexual and gender-based violence and have an equal opportunity to participate in education and the broader society.

Our expertise

Family Lives brings together our experience of working with families and with young people in schools to call for action by government, schools and families. In September 2011, Family Lives merged with the charity Teen Boundaries. Teen Boundaries began as the only charity solely devoted to stopping sexual bullying and encouraging positive gender relationships. The project aims to support schools and community groups in delivering high-quality Personal, Social, Health Education (PSHE) and Sex and Relationships Education (SRE).

The view from families: a survey of parents and children

In May 2011, Family Lives and alcohol awareness charity Drinkaware undertook a survey of 1002 parents of eight to 17 year olds and 633 ten to 17 year old children and young people to find out more about their attitudes to and experience of a range of issues, including their exposure to pornography, technology and the media. These results help to inform the analysis.

The sexualisation of mainstream culture and the danger of gender stereotypes

In common with the recent Bailey Review, many of the parents we surveyed are concerned about the effects of sexualised imagery and marketing, but we also found concern over the pressures of 'ideal' body images and gender stereotypes. Through our work with young people we know that negotiating sexualised and gender pressures in the teenage years can be very difficult. While research on the effects of sexualised media and marketing is mixed, it is clear that gender stereotyping has clear effects on development; potentially limiting girls' and boys' future aspirations and achievements, leading to associated social and educational costs.

Recommendation 1: Parents should be supported in reducing pressures for their children to conform to strict gender stereotypes. Retail codes of practice should contain guidance on good practice with regards to gender alongside sexualisation.

Recommendation 2: Schools should take a leading role in teaching children and young people to see through gender stereotypes and sexualised media from an early stage. Both primary and secondary schools should receive funding to invest in high-quality Personal, Social, Health Education (PSHE) lessons that explore gender stereotypes and help children to decode the messages that the media and marketing practices are sending about gender roles, empowering them to challenge what they see.

The importance of sex and relationship education: limiting the influence of pornography

Many parents, educators and policy makers continue to be concerned about children viewing pornography. This recently led to the Coalition Government putting out a consultation to introduce further regulations for Internet providers. Family Lives welcomes these proposals as the evidence shows that accidental exposure to pornography can be distressing for young children. However, there is a need to go further; research shows that increasing numbers of young people seek out explicit pornographic content and share this between them, subverting most parental and industry controls. A large reason for this is adolescents' curiosity and desire for frank information on sex. However, without educating young people about the unreality of pornographic sex through high-quality Sex and Relationship Education (SRE), there is a danger that young people will develop unhealthy and unrealistic expectations about sexual relationships.

Recommendation 3: The evidence shows that without access to information about sex and relationships, young people will rely on or be conditioned by inaccurate information or portrayals, including those from pornography. All schools, including primary schools should provide age appropriate Sex and Relationship Education (SRE).

Recommendation 4: Parents have a key role to play in reinforcing ideas about healthy relationships and sex. National awareness campaigns should be developed to up-skill parents to talk openly and confidently about sex and relationships to both boys and girls.

The digital world: new mediums for old risks

Digital and communication technologies are opening up children to new practices and pressures at a rate which leaves both parents and children struggling to fully recognise the potential risks and implications for the future. It is imperative that the ways in which children make use of new technology is known to parents and educators so that the potential risks, which include sexual exploitation, harassment and bullying, can be combated at the earliest available opportunity.

Recommendation 5: Many parents feel ill equipped to keep their children safe online and many others underestimate the risk to their child or the age at which their child may be engaging in risky or sexualised behaviour online. Support and awareness-raising campaigns targeted at parents may help to encourage them to talk to their children about staying safe in the digital world at an earlier stage, reducing their child's vulnerability to sexual exploitation.

Recommendation 6: All schools should be provided with guidance based on up-to-date research on pupils' evolving practices with regards to new digital and communication technologies. All schools should develop and update school policies which tackle new forms of bullying including sexual bullying and peer-on-peer sexual exploitation.

Hypermasculinity, gender violence and consent: a neglected issue

While many policy makers have been right to explore the nature of the growing sexualised and commercial pressures that young people face today, by framing the discussion around 'sexualisation and commercialisation' there is a potential that this debate can obscure or ignore another significant danger to the social, emotional and physical safety of young women and men: sexual harassment, bullying and assault by peers.

Recommendation 7: Urgent research is required to quantify the full extent of sexual violence between young people. Both quantitative and qualitative research is needed to explore the causal drivers underlying this behaviour. The Government should prioritise funding to ensure that there is enough data on this problem to understand the scale of the problem and generate evidence-based measures to tackle it.

Recommendation 8: Schools should play a leading role in teaching children and young people about consent and

unacceptable sexual behaviour, and should work with parents to ensure that these messages are delivered and reinforced in the home environment. Educational prevention initiatives must focus on teaching boys about consent and boundaries as well as girls.

All of our responsibility: the need for a whole-school approach

Family Lives considers the most effective strategy to address the continuing pressures that young people face today is to adopt a holistic, whole-school approach. However, recent policy with regards to tackling sexual bullying is fragmented and as such there is a danger that schools will not be able to fully address the commercialised, sexualised, gendered pressures that young people face today. In addition, there is a risk that sexual coercion and exploitation will not be systematically tackled.

Recommendation 9: In order to meet the Home Office's 'Preventing Violence Against Women and Girls' Strategy' there is a clear need for a consistent, universal approach in schools to ensure that all children and young people have the opportunity to realise their fullest social and intellectual potential and live lives that are free from coercion, exploitation and abuse. It is critical that the Department for Education are brought into these plans, as tackling child exploitation, violence against women and girls and empowering young people to resist sexualised and commercial pressures depends upon engaging schools and families. Family Lives recommends that the Department for Education should work towards producing guidance that supports a whole-school approach to tackle sexist, sexual and gender-based bullying.

June 2012

⇨ Information from Family Lives. Please visit www.familylives.org.uk for further information.

Sexualisation of children – protecting innocence online

At long last there is a reality check going on about the dangers children face on the Internet from pornography.

By Pippa Smith

We read with horror of children as young as eight admitting to pornography addiction, or the 12-year-old boy who raped a nine-year-old girl because he wanted to 'feel grown up' after viewing explicit images. As with so many other things in life, it has had to reach crisis-point before people begin sitting up and taking notice.

Only last week the deputy children's commissioner, Sue Berelowitz, told MPs that online porn 'is turning children into sex attackers, that the young act out depraved scenes they see on the web and there isn't a town, village or hamlet in which children are not being sexually exploited.'

This came in the same week that Wikipedia's co-founder Mike Sanger, disclosed that 'Wikipedia features some of the most disgusting sorts of porn you can imagine,' 'while being heavily used by children.'

The awful thing is that once children see these images they are imprinted on their brains. Dr William Struthers, a neuroscientist and expert in sexual arousal who researches the impact of pornography on young people, said, 'You can't 'un-see' something. These images are not easily erasable and become almost tattooed on the cortex. It is a powerful shock to the system.' He describes his research in his book, *Wired for Intimacy: How Pornography Hijacks the Male Brain.*

In November 2010, Safermedia's Parliamentary Conference on the harm that pornography does heard evidence of growing exposure to Internet porn and concomitant harm to children and adolescents from several expert speakers, including Pamela Paul, US journalist and author of Pornified.

Since then we have been running our Block Porn Campaign which backs Claire Perry MP's ideas for making the Internet safer for children. The recommendations of her parliamentary inquiry (supported by over 60 MPs) into online child protection are the way forward. These include a proposal for a formal consultation on the introduction of an opt-in network-level filtering system for all Internet accounts.

The default setting for pornography would be 'off', and it would be restored only after strict age verification for those over 18. This therefore is not censorship, despite howls of protest from some quarters about freedom of speech, and offers the best protection for children.

Network-level filters are particularly important as most parents are just not up to speed with the pace of technological change or the type of hardcore, violent and abusive material their children can now access. With the best will in the world many struggle to install device-level filters and are lagging behind their tech-savvy children. The problem will only get worse with the proliferation of the latest must-have smartphones being used by children.

So far TalkTalk (with a female CEO) is the only ISP which is delivering a package that filters at network level, although the default is still on and parents have to choose to block pornographic content. TalkTalk have also recently decided to extend this service to all their existing customers, not just new ones as is the case with the other large ISPs such as BT, Virgin Media and Sky who are not catching the 70% of existing customers.

Sue Berelowitz has backed the proposal for ISP-level filters with an 'opt in' for pornography; Mike Sanger is calling for Wikipedia to install a filter to protect children and now Louis Theroux has also added his voice to the need for network-level filters. So pressure is mounting on the ISPs to do the right thing and put children's safety and well-being ahead of profits.

19 June 2012

⇨ The above information is from *The Huffington Post* and is reprinted with kind permission from AOL (UK). Please visit www.huffingtonpost.co.uk for further information.

Hidden tide of child-on-child sex attacks

Internet pornography and the fashion for sexually explicit mobile phone messages could be fuelling a hidden tide of child-on-child rape and sexual assault, a report warns today.

By John Bingham

Evidence is mounting that the true scale of sexual violence among children could be far higher than previously thought, according to the charity Family Lives.

Parents and schools are failing to keep track with new trends in technology which are putting young people in danger not just from strangers but also their own peers, it warns.

An often-ignored culture of 'hypermasculinity' among boys is increasingly encouraging the view that violence against girls is acceptable or that scantily clad women 'deserve' to be raped, it adds.

'Girls as young as 11 are being coaxed by teenage boys into taking part in intimate webcam sessions'

Meanwhile girls as young as 11 are being coaxed by teenage boys into taking part in intimate webcam sessions using social networking sites without their parents' knowledge, it found.

Only a fraction of parents have spoken to their children about the dangers of digital sexual abuse, the research shows.

'Only a third of parents have spoken to their children about pornography'

The study follows a landmark government-backed report on the sexualisation and commercialisation of childhood by Reg Bailey, the chief executive of Mothers' Union last year which raised concerns that children are being pressurised to grow up too fast.

His report prompted retailers to promise to stop selling 'sexy' underwear to children and Ofcom, the broadcast regulator, to pledge to tighten up its use of the watershed.

But the Family Lives report warns that the previous emphasis on girls could be obscuring dangerous new trends among boys, with an emphasis on violence against other children.

It follows evidence to MPs last week by Sue Berelowitz, the Deputy Children's Commissioner, about a gang rape of a young girl by boys aged 14 and 15 who were summoned to take part using Blackberry messages.

'There is a great lack of accurate and up-to-date information on the prevalence of youth sexual violence, especially upon younger age groups; hence it is easy to simply dismiss the issue as extremely rare,' the report warns.

'However, from our work ... we know that this is a growing problem and as more cases of early sexual violence appear and throw light on the problem of peer-on-peer abuse, it is important to highlight this seldom discussed problem and work towards measures to tackle it.'

The report highlights accounts from parents including a father who was horrified to discover his 11-year-old daughter had been having sexually explicit exchanges with a 14-year-old boy online.

'From what I can tell she has showed him parts of her body on a webcam and possibly sent him photos of herself,' he said.

'I was extremely shocked to find this out as she has shown no interest in boys/sex/kissing, etc.

'But reading through the message history that I have found she has been discussing sex with him. She has also accessed porn sites.'

A mother also described how she discovered her teenage son had been involved in what she said amounted to 'cyber-sex'.

The report found that only a third of parents have spoken to their children about pornography and even fewer had tackled issues such as 'sexting' – sending sexually explicit images by text.

Claire Walker, head of policy at the charity, said: 'The scale of this is just not clear.

'The Government needs to commission some pretty solid research that looks at what is the extent.

'We know that hypermasculinity seems to be on the increase and one of the traits of it is peer-on-peer violence but all the evidence about hypermasculinity at the moment comes from America.

'Some of the things that we are aware of going on such as sexting and digital abuse – this is not just in urban schools or in state schools it is everywhere.

'Teachers don't always know how to deal with it and parents, on the whole, probably don't know it is going on.'

27 June 2012

⇨ The above article originally appeared in *The Telegraph* and is reprinted with permission. Please visit www.telegraph. co.uk for further information.

Ex 'lads' mag' editor: I regret my part in normalising porn

A former 'lads' mag' editor has spoken of his shame for defending the publication which he now believes encouraged young men to access hard core pornography.

Martin Daubney, who edited *Loaded* magazine for eight years, said becoming a father and turning 40 radically changed the way he looked at things.

Now he is concerned about an 'emotional time-bomb' for the next generation of young men as children get desensitised by online access to pornographic images.

Change

Mr Daubney took over at *Loaded* in 2002. He said his magazine gave its readers exactly what they wanted but 'the more we gave them, the more they demanded – and the racier we had to become in order to satiate their desires'.

He said that he became a 'skilled defender of the indefensible' as he took on critics of his publication.

But the former *Loaded* editor said his life 'changed for ever' when he became a father in 2009. 'A month later,' he added, 'I turned 40. Almost overnight, my world view changed.'

Dabble

He commented: 'I started seeing the women in my magazine not as sexual objects, but as somebody's daughter.'

And Mr Daubney, who became a stay-at-home father after leaving the magazine in 2010, went on: 'I was confronted by the painful thought that maybe *Loaded* was part of the problem.

'Was it an "enabler" to young teenage boys who'd consume harder porn later, in the same way dabbling with cannabis might lead to stronger addictions to cocaine or heroin?'

Regret

Mr Daubney added: 'Now, nearly two years on, I am ashamed at the way I used to defend my magazine.

'Offering excuses for pornography when *Loaded* was attacked left me feeling cheap and hollow. I became a person I wasn't, and, looking back, one I didn't like. Today, I find myself agreeing with some of my fiercest former critics.'

Mr Daubney admitted: 'We were normalising soft porn, and in so doing we must have made it more acceptable for young men to dive into the murky waters of harder stuff on the Internet. And, for that, I have a haunting sense of regret.'

13 June 2012

⇨ The above information is reprinted with kind permission from The Christian Institute. Please visit www.christian.org. uk for further information.

© The Christian Institute

Over one in five UK Children view 'inappropriate content' on their smartphones

A study, compiled by YouGov for Carphone Warehouse has found that 21% of eight to 15-year-olds in the UK have accessed 'inappropriate content' from their mobile phone.

By Art Modos

The investigation into the mobile web behaviour of eight to 15 year-olds in the UK found that 2.8 million or 25% of UK children aged eight to 12 have smart-phones, and more than one in five of those children admitted to accessing websites that they know are 'not for them'. However, answers to other questions in study indicate that this number may be higher with 87% saying they know that they do not have parental restrictions on their mobile phones.

Other possibly interesting stats are that the number of children watching 'online videos or video clips' on their mobile phones has more than doubled from 15% in 2008 to 36% in 2011. Carphone Warehouse says this makes it the second most popular online mobile activity, behind playing games.

It is unclear what exactly is meant by 'inappropriate content' and what the breakdown of that content would be, e.g. how much of it was 15+ certificated films (not likely to be high on smartphones) or other violent videos or games is completely unrevealed in the press coverage. However, it seems reasonable to assume that a significant portion of the number of eight to 15 year-olds who have seen 'inappropriate content' have seen porn.

This, I'm afraid, is just another phenomenon on a continuation that is seeing more and more children given private access to the web. For a while already many of those who can afford it have given their children laptops or a cheaper equivalent (netbooks). Kids are naturally curious and with our society so obsessed with sex (advertising for one...) it can't be long before they naively type away in Google to look for answers. What they find is porn.

I hate the way that so many news vendors aim to create fear in their readers, and some publications will use a story like this one to create fear of a new, morally void world of dangerous and uncontrollable technology. Despite this, it has to be acknowledged that there is a real problem. Porn can play an incredibly damaging role in the formation of children's sexuality and ideas about women and gender roles in general.

Now I'm of course not saying that we should fear tech, but we shouldn't be so naive about it either. It's naive to think (as some do) that it can be solved just by having web security, particularly because it's also naive to think that kids won't actively search for 'sex' online. It's also naive to think that porn is just pictures of sex, and that it won't try and make a bid early on for children's sexuality, the sexuality of their next customers. But perhaps most of all it's naive to think that we can allow porn to be the most prominent representation of sex in our culture and not expect problems?

1 February 2012

⇨ The above information is reprinted with kind permission from Carphone Warehouse. Please visit www. carphonewarehouse.com for further information.

Parents feel unable to protect children from inappropriate images

Information from OnePoll Data Hub.

By Sarah Laughran

Following a recent report that was commissioned by the Government, regarding the commercialisation and sexualisation of childhood (*Letting Children be Children*), politicians are now looking to discuss restrictions for music DVDs and videos. They will look at whether music DVDs should have ratings like those of films and if online music videos should have warnings of explicit content.

Head of the Mothers' Union, Reg Bailey conducted the report, which highlighted that parents are worried about protecting their children from inappropriate images as they are so widely available.

'62% of parents think lyrics in songs are too sexually explicit'

OnePoll conducted a survey on 1,000 parents with children under the age of 18 across the UK to find out their opinions on placing ratings on music DVD's and warnings on online music videos. Our survey aimed to find out how exposed parents thought their children were to inappropriate images and whether they thought music should be subject to a watershed.

Key results

⇨ 68% think music DVDs should have film-style age ratings

⇨ 74% think online music videos should have warnings if they contain explicit content

⇨ 74% think warnings and ratings would help protect children from content that they should perhaps not be looking at.

Protective parents

Shockingly, six out of ten parents do not feel able to protect their children from inappropriate images in music videos and DVDs. While 18% make sure every video their children watch is suitable, 46% say they try to monitor what their children watch but can't be with them all the time. A further 16% admit they can't stop them watching videos as they are so easily available. The government is now talking about there being a way for parents to filter out music and videos which are aimed at an older audience and 72% of parents we surveyed agree with this.

Watershed

Currently, music videos can be shown on television at any time of the day, and with widely accessible music channels, they are often easily available for children to watch. Watershed restrictions state that programmes broadcast between 5.30am and 9pm must be suitable for children, which rules out programmes that contain violence, intimidation, sex, and various other images.

At present, these restrictions do not apply to music videos which sometimes have content that, if in a film, would only be broadcast after 9pm. We asked parents if they thought that certain music videos should be included in watershed restrictions and 71% agreed.

Radio does not, at present, have a watershed, and programmes scheduled are based on who the presenters expect the audience to be. As 62% of parents that we surveyed think currently lyrics in songs are too sexually explicit, 66% think certain songs should only be played on radio after a certain time. When asked what time they think this should be;

⇨ 36% think after 9pm

⇨ 18% think after 8pm

⇨ 12% think after 10pm.

How would children feel about these restrictions?

The majority (43%) think children would find ways to watch the videos regardless of what restrictions the government attempted to put in place. However, over a third think they wouldn't notice they were being restricted and 17% think they would understand that it is not appropriate for them to watch those types of videos.

'68% think music DVDs should have film-style age ratings'

It appears that the majority of parents believe that their children are being exposed to too much adult content in songs and videos as the report suggests. They do want restrictions, ratings and warnings to help protect children from potentially distressing images as it is near impossible to make sure that minors do not access unsuitable images all of the time. With music videos not subject to watershed rules, but containing similar images found on television shows and films, it poses the question; why do they not come under watershed restrictions?

15 May 2012

⇨ The above information is reprinted with kind permission from OnePoll. Please visit www.onepoll.com for further information on this and other subjects.

A lack of clothes is not the problem with music videos today

A newly released report says videos with scantily clad women or 'sexual posing' should be relegated till after the watershed. How about insisting on decent storylines instead?

Hurray! The ruination of childhood innocence and degradation of society in general can, it seems, be slowed after all, by prudent scheduling, and/or Lady Gaga putting a nice big woolly jumper on.

Videos featuring underdressed women or 'sexual posing' should be kept off television screens until after the watershed, according to recommendations in a report written by Dr Linda Papadopoulos, a noted television-friendly celebrity psychologist. The report also seems to suggest that young people watch up to two and a half HOURS of music videos a day, which certainly raises more questions about effective time management – and how they can possibly find that volume of music video on television these days – than possible early-sexualisation.

Yes, there are many videos where women are objectified, represented as prey or easy pickings, or as something as commonplace and moist and underclothed as a mostly-peeled overripe satsuma. But to suggest the solution to this is blanket bans and sweeping overstatements is ridiculous. Singling out videos with skimpily clad women doesn't only affect the backing dancers of particularly misogynistic rap promos. Wouldn't the iconic video for Kylie Minogue's *Can't Get You Out of My Head* fit that bill too? And most of Madonna's videos? What about Beyonce? She's usually quite well covered, but in things so super-skintight that you can just about make out the outline of her appendix. Shouldn't artists be able to appear just as they damned well please? Or should all female artists risk nothing greater than a Victorian-baiting flash of ankle from now on?

What is this 'sexual posing' that is referred to? And who gets to decide what's sexy and what isn't?

Because, really, if the problem is that the songs that the videos are promoting are themselves sexual, why target the end product rather than the radio stations and record companies that market these artists and songs to the public – rather than the songs that deal in safer subject matters, like bunny rabbits and breakfast cereal.

Sex and music are intertwined – sex and music videos are too. And while this clearly doesn't mean that all promo videos should be shots of the Pussycat Dolls rubbing body glitter on their inner thighs (particularly if the video is publicising, say, the new Coldplay single), it's equally naive to think you can separate sex and the music video world entirely.

The main problem with music videos these days is that they tend to be lazy, turned out as an afterthought with a ridiculous lack of imagination and quality control. With most of the young people watching music videos they find on the Internet, record companies seem to think that – since people will have come looking for them anyway – there's no real reason to impress them once they've found it.

Which is just rubbish. And dangerous. Because teaching children that there's no point in trying is surely as dangerous as teaching them that having a firm, rounded bottom like two bald men hugging should be their natural expectation in life, isn't it? Well, almost as dangerous, then.

And once you decide that all artists (particularly female ones) should be allowed to wear whatever they want, and that the problem is not with the end product but with the general malaise of music – and that there are precious few music videos pre- OR post-watershed so it's all much of a muchness anyway – it is easy to decide on some new recommendations instead of these silly quotable but illogical and unworkable ones.

1. Make better music videos

2. Make them with storylines and coherent structure. Make them things that are good, not just things that are a duplicate of every other video of their genre.

3. Be innovative. If music videos (all two and a half hours of them per day) are so very influential, at least you could help children think of things in a new and exciting way.

4. All artists and their bands are only allowed the same amount of material in their costume as the most skimpily dressed dancer in their video.

5. For every video that a band and/or artist makes involving suggestions of sex, they must make three involving one or all of: committed loving relationships, career advice, responsible pet-ownership.

6. Any suggestive contact between members of the opposite (or same) sex must be played by people the same age and physical attractiveness of the target market's parents.

That should do it.

1 March 2010

⇨ Information from *The Guardian.* Please visit www.guardian.co.uk.

X Factor judge says music videos are too sexualised

Information from The Christian Institute.

Gary Barlow says music videos are too sexual, and he has had to shield his young children from sexualised pop images.

The X Factor judge, father of three and Take That star also warned about music lyrics which contain swearing.

Mr Barlow told *OK!* magazine: 'The other day I wanted some music in the kitchen and put on one of the music TV channels and a video came on which was so rude I had to turn it off because my nine-year-old was with me.'

Children

He commented: 'Don't get me wrong, I'm not a prude but I don't think I really want my children who are nine, 11 and two seeing these kind of videos at that age. I'm a parent.

'I have responsibility, but I also understand these videos are sexual to attract peoples' attention.'

The star also commented that he was unhappy when children being looked after by him sang songs which included inappropriate lyrics.

Faux porn

Mr Barlow said while his band's 'tours and some of our songs can be dressed a little sexually', it is 'not too in your face'.

In June Richard Russell, a music executive whose record company backs the hugely successful singer Adele, criticised the 'faux porn' imagery in music videos.

Last month a leading head teacher warned of 'an avalanche of images and malign influences' which is overwhelming young people.

Safeguard

Dr Helen Wright commented that now, 'more than ever', children 'are assaulted by inappropriate images everywhere they look – from the Internet, to the pages of magazines, to billboards, to displays in shops'.

Dr Wright, President of the Girls' Schools Association, continued: 'What hope have we got of safeguarding our children's sacred childhood if they are knocked off their feet on the nursery slopes of life by an avalanche of images and malign influences?'

5 December 2011

⇨ The above information is reprinted with kind permission from The Christian Institute. Please visit www.christian.org.uk for further information on this and other subjects.

Teenage sexting

According to Beatbullying, sexting has become an 'epidemic' among British teenagers.

By Rune H. Rasmussen

'It's so commonplace that I doubt many [teenagers] would bat an eyelid,' 16-year-old Amy said to the Telegraph. 'If I asked around, I could probably get ten to 20 photos that have been sent around or put on Facebook in under an hour.'

A widespread phenomenon

Sending sexually explicit photos, messages or video clips – or, as it is called, sexting – via mobile phones or the Internet, is becoming increasingly common among British teenagers. According to Sherry Adhami, Director of Communications at the charity Beatbullying, sexting has become an 'epidemic':

''We're seeing it more and more – we've even seen it in primary schools. It's 100 per cent classless; this affects children whether they're in deprived or affluent areas.'

Back in 2009, when Beatbullying polled 2,000 children, the results showed that a third of children had received a sexually explicit message online, while 25 per cent had received an image. Recent research from Plymouth University reveals that 40 per cent of 14- to 16-year-olds say they have friends who have engaged in sexting. Even more worrying, 20 per cent expressed that there was nothing wrong with full nudity in such messages, while 40 per cent said topless pictures were acceptable.

Coerced into sharing pictures

Exploring one's sexuality is a natural part of teenage life; however, the development of digital media has resulted in a new kind of cyberbullying, and experts fear that many young people are being coerced into providing explicit photos online. Sharing a sexual picture without consent via phones

and the Internet is a phenomenon coined as 'doxing'.

'For the first time in human history, everyone has got a camera in their pocket,' said Jonathan Baggaley of the Child Exploitation and Online Protection Centre (CEOP). 'And with apps like Instagram you can share a picture across multiple platforms at the click of a button.'

Jon Brown of the NSPCC, told the *Telegraph* that it is very often girls who are pressurised into exposing themselves:

'Girls feel coerced into sharing pictures. Boyfriends normalise it – it's the whole "If you really love me" argument. And it's often basic sexism, with girls being seen as boys' property. We've seen pictures where girls write across their breasts "I belong to X [the boyfriend's name]".'

Tink Palmer of the Marie Collins Foundation (MCF), a charity that helps young people who have suffered digital abuse, said:

'Girls aged 12 to 14 are naturally experimenting in many aspects of their life – with one, of course, being sex. When it comes to

sex online, the opportunities to [experiment] are greater and there is little parental control. [Teenagers] rarely give a second thought to the implications of their behaviour.'

The Logan case

One of the most profiled and serious sexting cases concerned 18-year-old Jessica Logan from Ohio. She sent her boyfriend a nude photo, but after they broke up he sent the picture to all of their friends, causing her to be labelled a 'slut', 'skank' and 'whore'. After months of tormenting, she hanged herself, leaving the phone in the middle of the room.

Professor Andy Phippen, who led the research at Plymouth University, claims that the Logan case 'shows that sexting and doxing can't be dismissed as youthful hijinks', and adds:

'We also have to be concerned that normal behaviour is being distorted. What happens when these people grow up? They need to understand that if they fancy a colleague, for example, they ask them out for a drink – they don't send them an explicit picture of themselves.'

Putting themselves at risk

Jonathan Baggaley of the CEOP thinks the rise in accessible online pornography, and the influence of such material, is to blame for the increase in sexting, saying that young men often believe that pornographic scenarios are the same as normal sexual behaviour. He also warns that young people are putting themselves at risk from child sex offenders, as webcams are increasingly being used for sexual experimentation.

'Child sex offenders are no longer looking to meet up, as they can abuse victims via a webcam,' said Baggaley. 'There's not even the traditional grooming process – we see abusers simply resorting to blackmail – recording a webcam feed (or pretending to) and then saying that they will send it to all the child's friends if the child doesn't do more extreme acts.'

Young people need guidance

'It's about being there to support your children if it does happen,' said Phippen, 'but also being responsible – not using computers and mobile phones as an electronic nanny, and thinking about restricting time online after 10pm.'

Brown added: 'Teachers also tell us that they're not sufficiently trained – that they need help. The Government and industry, who are raking in millions through smartphones, should take a lead role in bringing in a clearer set of guidelines on the use and abuse of such phones.'

'We need young people to realise that if you take an indecent picture of an under-18, you are breaking the law,' said Baggaley in conclusion. 'And while they might be happy sharing a picture with their boyfriend or girlfriend, they should know a large amount of this self-taken material ends up in the collections of child sex offenders. Finally, is it something they'd be happy with their mother or grandmother seeing?'

24 April 2012

⇨ The above information is reprinted with kind permission from KidsandMedia UK. Please visit www.kidsandmedia.co.uk for further information.

'Sexting' may be just a normal part of dating for Internet generation

Information from the University of Michigan.

For young adults today who were weaned on iPods and the Internet, the practice of 'sexting,' or sending sexually explicit photos or messages through phones, may be just another normal, healthy component of modern dating.

University of Michigan researchers looked at the sexting behavior of 3,447 men and women age 18-24 and found that while sexting is very common, sexting isn't associated with sexually risky behaviours or with psychological problems.

The findings contradict the public perception of sexting, which is often portrayed in the media and elsewhere as unsavoury, deviant or even criminal behaviour, said Jose Bauermeister, an assistant professor at the U-M School of Public Health and co-principal investigator of the study.

However, most of those negative stories involve sexting among pre-teens and teenagers, and the U-M study group was considerably older, said study co-author Debbie Gordon-Messer.

'For younger age groups, legality is an issue,' Gordon-Messer said. 'They are also in a very different place in their sexual development.'

This is the first known study to connect sexting with a behavioural outcome, Bauermeister said. Previous studies on sexting focus on demographic; in other words, who is doing the sexting, not how sexting impacts the health of the participants.

The researchers found that nearly half of the study respondents participated in sexting. Most people who reported receiving 'sexts' also reported sending them, which suggests that sexting is reciprocal and likely happens between romantic partners.

The researchers asked study participants about the number of sexual partners with whom they have had unprotected sex. The participants who 'sexted' did not report riskier sexual behavior than those who didn't. Nor did they report more depression, anxiety or low self-esteem, Bauermeister said.

In the larger picture, the sexting research is a very important piece of understanding how technology impacts sexuality and health, Bauermeister said.

'We have to keep paying attention to how technology influences our lives, including our sexuality and our sexual behaviour,' he said.

The study, *Sexting Among Young Adults* was produced jointly by the Sexuality and Health Lab, which Bauermeister directs, and the Prevention Research Center of Michigan, led by Marc Zimmerman, co-principal investigator on the study and a professor of public health and psychology. The U-M School of Public Health houses both centres. Alison Grodzinski of the Prevention Research Center of Michigan is also a co-author.

24 July 2012

⇨ Information from the University of Michigan. Please visit www.ns.umich.edu.

Web providers offer parents option to block porn

Four leading Internet service providers will offer customers the option to block adult content at the point of subscription.

By Rune H. Rasmussen

BT, Sky, TalkTalk and Virgin all offer parental control software that enables parents to keep their children away from adult content, violence and other inappropriate content. However, as only a minority of parents use the web filters, a new measure will be introduced to give parents more control.

Starting in 2012, all four leading Internet service providers will make sure that anyone signing up to a new broadband deal will have to choose whether or not they want to turn on parental control software, so that access to certain websites is blocked.

Concerns over sexualisation of children

The new measure is introduced as a result of the rising concerns regarding the increasing sexualisation of children through the media, following The Bailey Review, which was published earlier this year by the Christian charity Mothers' Union.

The four ISPs said in a statement that they 'have worked closely with government and a range of stakeholders to swiftly introduce measures addressing recommendations set out in the Bailey Review'.

TalkTalk's HomeSafe service

According to TalkTalk, 150,000 customers have so far opted in to their HomeSafe service, which blocks a variety of websites, including suicide and self-harm, violence and weapons, dating sites, gambling sites and filesharing. Parents have control over which sites are blocked by including them on a blacklist.

As well as this, TalkTalk offers network-level filtering software, which means that all devices used on the home Internet connection are protected, including laptops, tablet computers and smartphones.

No fool-proof solution

Critics have argued that web filters are not an ideal solution, as they sometimes block access to innocent websites and never will be able to shield people from all inappropriate sites.

'It's worth noting that those determined to get around a filter will find a way of doing so, often quite trivially,' said Sebastien Lahtinen from Think Broadband to the BBC.

As well as this, children may access the Internet from a variety of devices, and there are certainly ways to do so without logging on to the home Internet connection.

The most important filter is in our minds

For this reason, it's important to remember that the most important filter isn't on your computer, but in the heart and the mind of the user. As parents, the most important task of all is to create a healthy attitude in our children, to regularly talk to them about media use in general, and to agree on a set of rules that are to be followed.

23 September 2011

⇨ The above information is reprinted with kind permission from KidsandMedia UK. Please visit www.kidsandmedia.co.uk for further information.

Internet porn petition will reach the Government with 100,000 signatures

Information from The Huffington Post.

A petition demanded Internet providers to block access to hard core pornography by default will be handed into the Government on Thursday with over 100,000 signatures.

The 'Safetynet' petition, which has been signed by 110,000 people including peers, MPs and religious figures, asks Internet service providers such as BT, Sky and Virgin to cut off access to adult content on computers and mobile phones.

Premier Christian Media, the organisation behind the petition, has called on the Government to 'take decisive action to halt this blatant and relentless assault on young and impressionable minds'.

Peter Kerridge, their chief executive, said: 'This simple measure would in no way restrict adults from accessing such websites by specific application but would help to protect generations of young people from online pornographers.'

'We demand that they lock this ever-open door to pornography and depravity once and for all.'

The petition, which takes the form of a letter to the now-former Culture Secretary Jeremy Hunt, claims one in three ten-year-olds have 'stumbled upon pornography', and that the single largest consumer group of Internet porn are children aged 12 to 17.

In June the Government launched a ten-week consultation asking parents and businesses for their views on the best way to shield children from Internet pornography.

The study is also looking at measures to protect children from other potentially harmful sites such as those which promote suicide, anorexia, gambling, self-harm and violence.

> **'Parents are being asked for their views on three possible systems, including one where users have to "opt in" to see adult sites'**

Views on preventing online sexual grooming and cyber-bullying are also being sought, the DfE said when it was launched.

Parents are being asked for their views on three possible systems, including one where users have to 'opt in' to see adult sites, and one in which customers are presented with an unavoidable choice about whether they want filters and blocks installed.

The third option would combine the two systems, enabling customers to block some content automatically and be given a choice to unblock them as they wish.

It comes after David Cameron said earlier this year that the Government needed to look at whether Internet services or devices might come with a filter on as their default setting or have a combination of a filter and an 'active choice' by the customer.

4 September 2012

⇨ The above information is from *The Huffington Post* and is reprinted with permission from AOL (UK). Please visit www.huffingtonpost.co.uk for further information.

French report calls for end to sexualisation of children

Former minister wants ban on beauty contests for under-16s and children's lingerie in wake of ten-year-old's *Vogue* spread.

By Kim Willsher

A French Government report is calling for a ban on 'mini-miss' beauty pageants and children's lingerie to combat what it describes as the 'hyper-sexualisation' of children.

The moves follow an international controversy over a *Vogue* magazine photographic shoot featuring provocative images of a ten-year-old French girl.

The parliamentary report, *Against Hyper-Sexualisation: A New Fight For Equality*, calls for a ban on child-size adult clothing, such as padded bras and high-heeled

shoes for children, and an end to beauty competitions for the under-16s.

Chantal Jouanno, the author of the report and a senator and former sports minister, has also called for the outlawing of young models in advertising campaigns and the return of uniforms in primary schools as part of a series of measures to stem the psychological damage she believes is being done to children.

Jouanno said young girls were being disguised as 'sexual candy' in a competition over appearance, beauty and seduction, which she said was 'contrary to the dignity of the human being' and a step backwards in the battle for sex equality.

'This phenomenon is a real concern for society,' Jouanno told *Le Figaro* newspaper. 'Today, children are building their identities amid a regression of sexual equality and on the return of stereotypes contained in music clips, games, reality

television programmes. The danger is not only individual but collective.

'We have a great responsibility as both politicians and parents.'

She argued that while the sexualisation of children is not widespread in France, it is increasing and becoming acceptable because of what she described as the insidious 'normalisation' of pornographic images.

The issue has also been taken up in Britain, Belgium and Quebec. A British report last year, *Letting Children be Children*, recommended excluding sexual imagery from children's daily lives by tighter controls on advertising and pre-watershed television schedules.

The French report was prompted by international outrage after publication of a multi-page feature in *Vogue*'s December 2010 issue in which ten-year-old Thylane Loubry Blondeau, and two other girls, were photographed pouting and posing heavily made up, with lipstick, tight dresses, jewels and high heels.

While the feature initially failed to rouse anger in France, it caused outrage in America where the pictures were considered inappropriate, prompting the

French Government to announce its inquiry.

Vogue defended the article, saying the young models were simply dressing up 'like maman', as all young girls do. Blondeau, whose mother is French actress turned designer Veronica Loubry and father former footballer Patrick Blondeau, has been modelling since she was five. Her mother, Loubry, defended the photographs in a blog at the time, writing: 'The only thing that shocks me about the photo is that the necklace she is wearing is worth three million euros ... my daughter isn't naked, let's not blow things out of proportion.'

The view was not shared by most French mothers; a survey carried out at the time of the controversy by the parenting website Magicmaman found 84% of those asked thought the images of Blondeau were demeaning.

The Government report, published on Monday, criticised the marketing of padded bras for eight-year-olds, thong underwear, make-up kits, and leggy dolls, all aimed at pre-pubescent girls under the age of 12.

Specialists involved in the research concluded that this precocious sexualisation affected mostly girls and caused 'psychological damage that is irreversible in 80% of cases'. At worse, said the report, it could result in eating disorders including anorexia.

As well as banning clothing and make-up considered inappropriate for young girls, Jouanno also proposes making it illegal for top fashion houses or companies to use models under 16 in their campaigns.

Reintroducing school uniforms was a way of combatting competition between pupils over fashion label clothes which highlight social inequalities, said the report.

6 March 2012

⇨ The above article originally appeared in the *Guardian* and is reprinted with permission. Visit www.guardian.co.uk for further information.

Mum dresses toddler up as a prostitute for beauty pageant

Information from parentdish.

By Kelly Rose Bradford

A 'pageant mom' dressed her three-year-old toddler up as a PROSTITUTE for a beauty competition. The little girl, Paisley, can be seen on tomorrow's episode of *Toddlers and Tiaras* taking off Julie Roberts' streetwalker character from the film, Pretty Woman.

In the video on Radaronline.com, the toddler is dressed in a clinging Lycra dress, wig, full make-up and thigh-high PVC boots, in scenes that will sicken many parents.

One appalled mum – whose own daughter was competing in the same pageant – goes on camera to express her shock, saying: 'I would never, ever do that to my little girl. Ever!'

The show faced a barrage of criticism last week when a four-year-old was shown dressed as Dolly Parton, complete with fake breasts and padded out buttocks. Some outraged viewers have even set up Facebook groups condemning the programme and calling for it to be taken off air.

7 September 2011

⇨ The above information is from parentdish and is reprinted with kind permission from AOL (UK). Please visit www.parentdish. co.uk for further information.

...AND I DON'T NEED TO KNOW WHAT A PROSTITUTE IS..?

UK beauty pageant for girls under 13 branded 'pointless' and 'tacky'…

Information from OnePoll Data Hub.

By Jessica Burnham

In a society where images of 'beauty' are depicted through the media on a daily basis, it is hardly surprising we are becoming a nation obsessed with our looks. Magazines inform us of the latest fashion trends, TV adverts which hair, make-up and body products to use, and giant billboards what type of body is now considered to be 'perfect'.

Following in the footsteps of America, however, with its TV series *Toddlers and Tiaras*, one can't help but wonder if we have now gone a step too far? In June, the city of Leicester will host the first ever beauty pageant for little girls. Entitled 'Miss Mini Princess UK' the contest is specifically for girls aged up to 13 and will involve judgements on physical beauty, an eye catching outfit, a talent, and finally poise in evening wear.

Despite the contest already being slated as a 'paedophiles paradise' and organisers receiving hate mail, Robyn Sutherland, mum of 23-month-old Eleanor June Rees-Sutherland, plans on entering her daughter into the competition. Robyn has been quoted saying she doesn't see what all the fuss is about, and can't understand what's wrong with making little girls look like a princess for the day. She says she enjoys dressing her daughter up and that Eleanor June loves make up too.

OnePoll asked a nationally representative sample of 1,000 UK adults what they thought about pageants, the associated risks, and whether it was appropriate for such young girls to be paraded and judged on their 'beauty'.

The results

The overall opinion of beauty pageants was negative with words such as 'pointless' and 'tacky' frequently being used to describe such events.

83% of adults said they didn't think beauty pageants should be available for girls of this age and 86% of respondents said they wouldn't let their daughter (aged 13 or under) in such a competition even if there was appropriate monitoring and security.

It would appear the majority of adults think the pageants are just too risky (78%) with the top three concerns being

⇨ Sexualisation of children 82%

⇨ Obsessive/Pushy parents 81%

⇨ Paedophile interest 72%

Furthermore, when asked what age they thought was appropriate for girls to start wearing make-up and fan tanning, etc. (procedures that are a 'necessity' for beauty pageants) the majority of respondents not only stated answers years ahead of Eleanor June, but also ages above 13 (the upper age threshold for the competition). Such findings suggest that adults think that the girls entering this pageant are simply too young to be 'beautified'.

Indeed, these stats appeared to be echoed in respondents' opinions on mum Robyn Sutherland – 81% of adults thought it was inappropriate for her to enter her daughter into the pageant. When asked why top answers included that Eleanor June was too young, and it wasn't her choice to enter. Respondents thought Eleanor should be left to be a child and not judged on her looks from such a young age. Such pageants were described to promote the sexualisation of children.

A key point to remember here is that it is not 'children' in these pageants – it is in fact just girls. Boys will not be part of this competition and do not typically feature in 'beauty pageants'. We asked respondents whether they thought beauty pageants should be available for boys/men?

⇨ 12% said 'Both boys and men'

⇨ 11% said 'No, they were only appropriate for girls/women'.

The majority of adults (68%), however, said 'No –– because they simply didn't agree with them altogether.'

It would seem therefore the general consensus on such competitions is that they are exploitative, pushing children to adopt semi-sexualised adult mannerisms that they do not fully understand and enforcing the message that appearance is everything. Those in the pageant industry, however, still seem to insist that it is all just harmless fun and that they believe the competitions instil girls with confidence and self-esteem.

13 June 2012

⇨ The above information is reprinted with kind permission from One Poll. Please visit www. onepoll.com for further information.

Child beauty shows? They're harmless fun blasts mum Gemma Blackhurst

A mum has hit back at critics of child beauty pageants – as her ten-year-old daughter prepares to take to the catwalk for the first time.

Gemma Blackhurst, 27, says the craze – which is a major industry in the US and is starting to grow in popularity in Britain – does not harm the girls who are transformed into 'mini adults'.

Child protection charities say the events sexualise and exploit youngsters, who pose in make-up, fake eyelashes and miniature ballgowns.

But mum-of-three Gemma, from Oldham, says daughter Brodie was so keen to learn how to perform she attended a bootcamp for young beauty queens.

The schoolgirl has entered a number of pageants over the summer, as well as the America Tots & Tiaras competition in Manchester in October.

Gemma said: 'I wouldn't make her do anything she didn't want to do.

'If she doesn't want to do it then that's fine, but at the moment she can't get enough of it.

'The UK pageants are nothing like the US with pushy mums forcing babies to wear make-up – I was surprised at how laid back it all is here.

'There are some younger children but most are Brodie's age upwards and they are there because they want to be.

'At the bootcamp, they were taught the "dos and don'ts" of how to put on make-up and taught poses. They were told to try and stay as natural as they can and don't have to have hair-pieces or fake tan and lashes.

'The children are only young and being natural is when they are the most beautiful.'

But Claude Knights, director of child protection charity Kidscape, blasted the pageants as being about the 'commercialisation and sexualisation of childhood' – giving girls the impression that it is fine for them to value themselves in a 'superficial' way.

The world of children's beauty pageants has been thrust into the spotlight by controversial American reality series *Toddlers & Tiaras*. The show has seen a three-year-old put in heels and told to 'strut' by her mum and a nine-year-old made to have her eyebrows waxed in a bid to win a title.

Brodie hopes to become a dressmaker and helps pick her outfits.

Gemma, also mum to Bailee, two, and four-year-old Madison, said preparing for the pageants had also allowed her to spend time with Brodie.

She said: 'This is something for me and Brodie and all the attention is on her. I'm not a girly girl but she's the complete opposite of me. It was all Brodie's idea and this is something she wants to get into.

'It's an expensive hobby but we work really hard. The pageant atmosphere is absolutely fantastic with a chance to make new friends and it's not at all competitive. Brodie has started to get a lot more confidence and I've seen a different side to her.'

13 July 2012

⇨ Information from the *Manchester Evening News*. Please visit www.menmedia.co.uk for further information.

Fury over Primark's padded bikinis for children

Information from the Press Association.

Retailer Primark has been accused of exploiting children over its decision to sell a padded bikini top for young girls.

Child protection consultant Shy Keenan, of The Phoenix Chief Advocates, which helps victims of paedophiles, said: 'It never fails to amaze me just how many High Street household names are now prepared to exploit the disgusting "paedophile pound".'

She added: 'You should never sexualise children.

'Kids may be learning how to look sexy in an adult way but no one is teaching them what to do if they receive unwelcome robust adult attention.'

Primark, which has 138 UK stores and 38 in Ireland, says on its website: 'Every girl wants to look her best and at Primark we make no exception for the younger ladies. All the high fashion trends can be found in our Girlswear section, no matter what age you are.'

Ms Keenan said The Phoenix Chief Advocates was urging shoppers to support its stance by refusing to spend their money at Primark.

'We say boycott Primark until they agree to withdraw this line,' she said.

People are also being urged to contact the company directly to ask that Primark seeks 'more informed advice' about the children's clothes which it stocks in future.

Primark is the latest chain to face criticism for selling products deemed too adult for young children.

Asda was criticised for selling lace lingerie, including a push-up bra, aimed at young girls and Tesco withdrew a pole-dancing kit which appeared in its toys section.

WHSmith announced last year that it was withdrawing Playboy stationery, including a pencil case, but refused to say if the decision was due to criticism about the brand being sold to schoolchildren.

Parents' networking website Mumsnet has launched a 'Let Girls Be Girls' campaign to let retailers know that parents do not want their children offered products which 'prematurely sexualise' them.

Brands which have signed up include George at Asda.

Prime Minister Gordon Brown also backed the campaign, saying 'all of us as parents can recognise there's something wrong when companies are pushing our kids into acting like little grown-ups when they should be enjoying being children'.

During his party's manifesto launch yesterday, Conservative leader David Cameron demanded social responsibility 'instead of businesses and media companies encouraging the premature sexualisation and commercialisation of childhood'.

14 April 2010

⇨ The above information is reprinted with kind permission from the Press Association. Please visit www.pressassociation.com for further information.

© 2010 Press Association

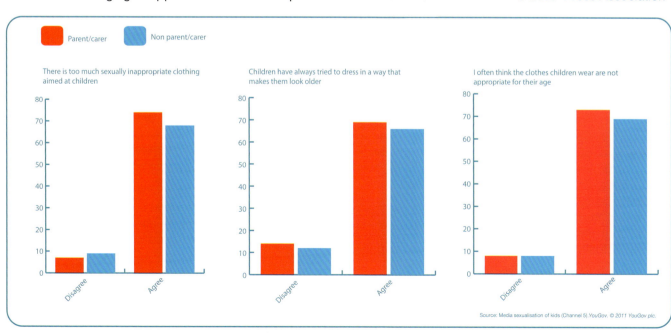

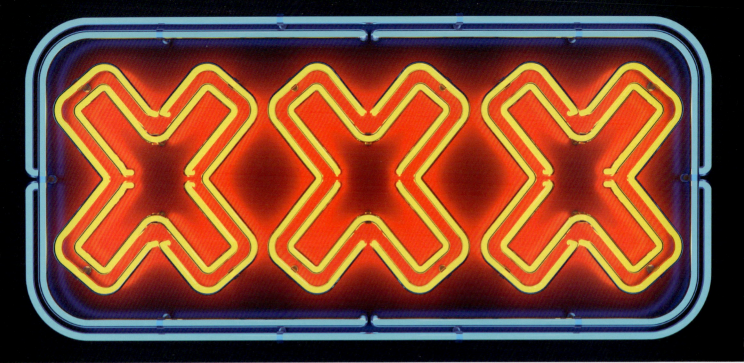

Hot pants or hot air?

Is the 'sexualisation of young girls' really getting worse – or has it been exaggerated for the sake of shocking tabloid headlines? Ruth Whippman reports.

I was a TV researcher for several years. As well as being mind-blowingly fascinating, it's a strange and often stressful job. You are, in effect, the personal concierge to the uniquely demanding creature that is the TV producer (I later became one of those too, so feel I can speak freely) and it is your job to fulfil his or her every creative whim.

'Sexualisation of children [is] a great vote-winner for politicians'

You must interpret the weird, cosmic ordering – 'I need a man who is so addicted to gambling he wears nappies! By five o'clock! Plus a kilo of moon rock!' – and bring back each bizarrely specific item on the list. Given that your job depends on it, you get pretty good at making items materialise out of thin air that one might have believed did not actually exist at all.

This is a skill that comes in particularly handy when the 'sexualisation of children' story rolls around again, usually in response

to another government review on the subject (there have been five separate reviews into this issue since 2008 – it's a great vote-winner for politicians).

Reading what the tabloids had to say on the matter, it would be easy to believe that Britain's high street was brimming with pint-sized prostitute apparel; that Bratz dolls were turning tricks on the shelves of Toys R Us and Matalan's childrenswear buyers were little better than a paedophile ring. So when your producer asks you to get hold of a few sleazy items for kids for a programme on the subject, it should be a doddle.

'I want crotchless knickers for four-year-olds!' I remember one producer bellowing. Mentally adjusting the request for legality and plausibility I would obediently trot off to the shops.

It allows the tabloids to adopt the tone at which they most excel: that of simultaneous sanctimony and titillation

And each time, the same thing would happen. After days of scouring the darkest corners of the

high street, I would draw a blank. Despite the compelling motivation of the TV researcher's crushing fear of failure, it was almost impossible to come up with a single item that even the most assiduous *Daily Mail* hack could get particularly worked up about.

'No Playboy t-shirts, or shockingly short skirts or black lace underwear for eight-year-olds anywhere in sight'

The children's sections of the shops were filled with jeans and t-shirts and leggings and plain white cotton training bras. No Playboy t-shirts, or shockingly short skirts or black lace underwear for eight-year-olds anywhere in sight.

In fact, the general landscape of creepiness seemed, if anything, to have gone down a notch since I was a kid back in the 1980s, when the sight of a five-year-old Sheena Easton impersonator in nightwear and full make-up, crooning 'night time is the right time...we make love' on prime-time television was considered a wholesome evening's viewing.

But instead of throwing our hands up in defeat and putting out a programme admitting that the whole issue had been exaggerated beyond all proportion, we would dredge up a couple of pairs of fishnets in a size extra-small from a market stall somewhere, that could possibly fit a largish eight-year-old with a bit of hoiking up, and maybe a couple of shortish skirts, and a Bratz doll or two, and would put it all together, throw in some shock-horror commentary and thus perpetuate the moral panic.

'The Bailey Review is a perfect example of how the pursuit of a tabloid-style moralising agenda can divert attention away from problems that are far more important'

The 'sexualisation of young girls' story is a favourite with the media (the observant among you will notice that there's a clue to this in the words 'sex' and 'young girls'.) It allows the tabloids to adopt the tone at which they most excel: that of simultaneous sanctimony and titillation, and gives everyone a free pass to show lots of pictures of teenagers in skimpy outfits.

Exaggeration and scaremongering are all very well when it comes to the tabloid press, but when this issue starts taking up a fair amount of valuable government time and resources then it starts to become a problem, especially when it starts to obscure other more real and pressing concerns.

As we gear up for yet another government 'crackdown' on child sexualisation, this has never been more in evidence. The policy recommendations unveiled to business leaders in Downing Street this year, were inspired by the findings of last year's Bailey Review commissioned by the Prime Minister, into the so-called 'commercialisation and sexualisation of childhood'.

The Bailey Review is a perfect example of how the pursuit of a tabloid-style moralising agenda can divert attention away from problems that are far more important.

The review was headed up by Reg Bailey, the CEO of conservative Christian charity, the Mothers' Union, whose work involves, in part, lobbying on this very issue (other projects include selling toys and other children's products on their website - nothing sexual of course, unless you happen to have a fetish for nursery prayer books). It was tasked with exploring all aspects of the commercialisation of childhood, including, but not exclusively the issue of sexualisation.

Given the work of Bailey's organisation, it would seem likely that he would be keen to pursue the sexualisation agenda at the expense of other concerns, and that is exactly what happened.

The unisex toys of my childhood have largely disappeared

At the outset of the review, Bailey's team asked parents what their most pressing concerns were for their children under the broad subject heading of the commercialisation of childhood. Predictably, given the media coverage given to the subject, and the general nature of the questioning, they mentioned sexualisation. But they also gave equal weight to another topic, one which is much less popular with the media.

The issue they mentioned repeatedly as being of particular concern, was that of gender stereotyping, in toys, products and marketing aimed at children.

Parents are right to be worried about this. Gender stereotyping in children's products in recent years has taken a leap into the realms of caricature.

Far from a steady march towards equality of the sexes, a segregation now exists that would have been considered laughable in my childhood in the 1970s and '80s. Walk into any toyshop (except the weird middle-class ones that only the sell the unidentifiable wooden

toys that your kids hate) and you will find a neon pink girls' section displaying a Lilliputian dystopia of domestic drudgery (hoover! Do laundry! Find fulfillment in childcare! Apply kiddie make-up to disguise the dark hollows under your eyes caused by valium addiction!) A slightly more fun but equally restrictive boys' section will offer up various miniaturised means of mass slaughter, with a handy selection of emergency vehicles to clean up the bloodshed. And social ridicule awaits children of either sex who break out of the shackles of their gender.

The unisex toys of my childhood have largely disappeared, with even Lego, the last bastion of Scandinavian common sense, recently releasing a range of pink and lavender Lego for Girls, complete with beauty-salon themed set.

A growing body of scientific research points to the fact that this type of gender stereotyping is harmful for children, impacting significantly on cognitive ability, confidence and life prospects as well as encouraging bullying and alienation for those who don't fit the bill.

'This type of gender stereotyping is harmful for children'

And, as pointed out by Meg Barker, senior lecturer in psychology at the Open University, unlike gender stereotyping, no corresponding research exists to demonstrate that sexualisation of children in products and clothing has long-term damaging effects.

Despite the claims of certain popular science authors, this growing gender divide is not about biology but about money. Treating boys and girls as entirely distinct groups of consumers – each needing their own complete colour-coded set of toys – can double sales.

Marketing executives are highly incentivised to exploit children's fledgling sense of gender identity to make them persuade their parents to part with their cash. This is certainly

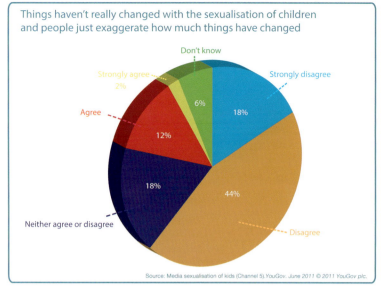

Things haven't really changed with the sexualisation of children and people just exaggerate how much things have changed

- Don't know
- Strongly disagree 18%
- Strongly agree 2%
- Agree 12%
- Disagree 44%
- Neither agree or disagree 18%
- 6%

Source: Media sexualisation of kids (Channel 5).YouGov. June 2011 © 2011 YouGov plc.

one of the clearest examples of the growing commercialisation of childhood, exactly the area that the Bailey Review was supposed to be exploring.

Despite this glaring truism, and the fact that parents cited gender stereotyping as a key concern, the Bailey Review managed to dispense with the issue with breathtaking dismissiveness.

Bailey concludes, contrary to the scientific evidence, that far from being the problem that silly old parents thought it was, gender stereotyping is actually 'healthy' for children.

The 99-page review document devotes just five paragraphs to the problem (although, to give Bailey credit, they punch above their weight – between the five of them they manage to pack in the full range of clichés, offensive stereotypes and cod-science commonly deployed on the subject).

Bailey starts with the tedious and largely discredited neuroscience argument, regurgitating the idea that gender differences are biologically driven and there ain't much that nurture can do about it (Cordelia Fine dismisses this myth particularly effectively with a meticulous look at the evidence in her book *Delusions of Gender*).

And then immediately contradicting his initial insistence that what we like and dislike is pre-ordained by our gender at birth, he then suggests that gendered marketing can indeed change behaviour, but...wait for it...

in a good way!

Girls who would not normally be able to handle something as difficult and as 'boyish' as science could, it turns out, grow to like it after all, as long as it was marketed to them in a pink package, as an activity that could encompass their true calling - that of beauty and pampering. (It's not quite clear how he squares his 'science is for boys' worldview with the fact that girls have long been outperforming boys in science at school.)

He then offers up a case study, provided by a toy manufacturer named Bob Paton, who states:

We were selling chemistry sets at a rate of 15,000 per annum, but when we put them in pink packaging and called it a craft activity sales went up to 80,000-120,000 sets per annum ever since!... Experience has taught us that the success or otherwise of a toy depends largely on... communicating quickly to the consumer whether a toy is best suited to boys or to girls.

Which seems to put Bailey in the unlikely position of defending gender stereotyping on the grounds that it furthers the noble cause of Helping Shops Sell More Stuff, a viewpoint one might think was a little out of place in a document that is supposed to be combatting the commercialisation of childhood. Incidentally, it would have made interesting reading had the same logic been applied to a case study in the 'sexualisation' section of the review, for example:

We were selling plain white cotton underwear for children, but were only shifting 15,000 units per annum. As soon as we shifted to black lace peephole bras our sales went up to 120,000 units per annum ever since!

Bailey finishes up his brief foray into this issue by concluding, contrary to the scientific evidence, that far from being the problem that silly old parents thought it was, gender stereotyping is actually 'healthy' for children and that no action should be taken on the matter. He then moves on from the issue with breakneck speed, devoting the rest of the 99 pages of his report to his pet cause and thereby crushing forever the fledgling hope that someone might somehow take a real look at how this problem might be tackled.

As well as it being amazing that such blatant sexism was allowed to pass through unquestioned in a 21st century government document, the Bailey Review is a real missed opportunity. As the captains of industry gather in a series of meetings at Downing Street to discuss Bailey's recommendations, this issue will not be on the table.

Gender stereotyping in marketing to children is one area which could truly benefit from some light regulation, or voluntary codes of practice, or at least a genuine discussion which looks objectively at the evidence of the harm this issue causes. If Bailey hadn't been so blinded by his own moralising agenda, things might have been different.

Image of the front page of the Bailey review, 'Letting Children be Children' in the public domain. Picture of an advert for dressing-up costumes shows a boy and girl wearing aprons, with the boy's apron reading 'Super Chef' and the girl's apron reading 'Super Cook.' Picture of an advert for boys and girls dressing-up trunks: boys' trunk is brown and contains costumes for pirates and cowboys, girls' trunk is pink and contains fairy costumes.

26 February 2012

⇨ Information from the F word. Please visit www.thefword.org.uk for more information.

© the F word

Sexualisation of childhood: Facebook and padded bras worry 90% of parents

Information from the Press Association.

Targeting children on Facebook and selling inappropriate products, such as padded bras, concerns almost 90% of parents, a study has revealed.

Nine in ten parents (90%) still think there are problems with the way some companies advertise to children and 85% are unaware of the dedicated complaints and advice website ParentPort, according to a poll for the Chartered Institute of Marketing (CIM).

'Targeting children on Facebook and in stores are significant concerns'

The survey comes a year after the report by Mothers' Union chief executive Reg Bailey, entitled *Letting Children Be Children*, which called on businesses and broadcasters to play their part in protecting young people from the 'increasingly sexualised wallpaper surrounding them'.

Parents remain most concerned about sexually explicit outdoor advertising, marketing during children's TV programmes and inappropriate products for children, such as padded bras, the poll says.

Targeting children on Facebook and in stores are other significant concerns.

The CIM is calling on the Government to work directly with the marketing industry to 'deal with these pressing issues once and for all'.

David Thorp, director of CIM research, said: 'It's clear that parents still have very real concerns about the way some companies try to sell to children. The marketing profession needs to address these concerns but we also want a dialogue between parents, the Government and industry bodies to ensure that our solutions are lasting and effective.

'The advertising that parents see and worry about is only the visible tip of the iceberg. Marketing runs much deeper and touches on every part of product development, buying and placement.

'Our research shows parents trust and respect the Advertising Standards Authority (ASA) as a regulatory body but the ASA is only able to tackle part of the problem. By looking at the often-invisible marketing decisions which lead to the creation of products like padded bras for children, we can treat the cause of the problem, not just the symptoms.

'We need to ensure that every decision that companies take about marketing to children is responsible and appropriate. Parents should never have to react to inappropriate marketing.

'The Chartered Institute of Marketing wants to sit down with the Government to provide clarity and leadership for the marketing profession.'

The ASA said: 'The work that regulators, including the ASA, continue to undertake in responding positively to the recommendations in the Bailey Review (*Letting Children Be Children*) has been welcomed by Government as well as family and parenting groups.

'ParentPort is a valued resource amongst parents but raising awareness is an ongoing process. We'd be delighted if CIM and its members would like to support ParentPort with their expertise and resources.'

'Parents remain most concerned about sexually explicit outdoor advertising'

A Department for Education spokesman said: 'Reg Bailey's recommendations have already prompted swift action from industry and regulators. Setting up the ParentPort website is just one of the steps they have taken. We want parents to use the website to give feedback, make complaints and learn more about media regulation, online safety and other aspects of the commercial world, like retailing, that have an impact on children.

'We look forward to working with the Chartered Institute of Marketing in exploring what more can be done to tackle the commercialisation and sexualisation of childhood.'

6 June 2012

⇨ Information from the Press Association. Please visit www.pressassociation.co.uk for further information.

Parents becoming complicit in the sexualisation of children

***Information from** The Huffington Post.*

By Shaista Gohir

Last week, four-year-old Maddy Jackson appeared on the US reality show *Toddlers and Tiaras* wearing a padded bra. Her mother also gave her a padded bottom and made her don a peroxide wig in an attempt to make her look like Dolly Parton. I am disgusted by this mother – the lengths that some people go to for a few minutes of fame has really hit an all time low. Where is Maddy's father – why is he not stopping this?

I am disturbed by some mothers in Britain too – the one who gives her 4 year old a spray tan, the one who teaches her 7 year old pole dancing and the one who injects her 8 year old with botox. And these are the cases that we know about through media. I wonder how many more parents are encouraging their little girls to grow up too quickly. Television, magazines, music and clothing are already sexualising children, so when mothers start joining in, then things have just gone too far!

At the other end of the spectrum, I am also troubled by a minority of conservative Muslim parents who are making girls as young as three, four and five wear hijabs (headscarves) despite it not being a religious obligation for them. It may be unintentional, but they are also sexualising their children because the purpose of the hijab is to prevent unwanted male sexual attention. By wrapping little girls in headscarves they are being treated as sex objects, who apparently need to be covered up. A healthy balance can be struck on children's appearance without going to such extremes.

Many of us would be critical of the parents mentioned so far. But how many of us are also sending the wrong messages to our children through inappropriate choices that we are making unconsciously. I blame the mothers because women are making majority of the purchasing decisions. They are buying high-heeled shoes, provocative underwear and sexy clothing. Kids wear adorned with slogans that are sexist or have sexual innuendoes are also regularly being bought. Here are some examples of the types of slogans that have appeared on girl tops: 'Future WAG', 'Future Porn Star', 'So Many Boys, So Little Time'. Babies have not been spared from sleaze either and wording has included, 'I love boobies' and 'Mother Sucker'. A couple of years ago there was outrage in New Zealand when babywear featured, 'I'm Living Proof My Mum is Easy', and 'The Condom Broke'. I know sex sells, but this is ridiculous!

'My best subjects are boys, shopping, music and dancing'

Last week, another T-shirt caused controversy for being sexist. It was covered with, 'I'm too pretty to do my homework so my brother has to do it for me.' JC Penney, a national retailer in the US, discontinued the 'Too pretty' T-shirt within 24 hours of a petition going viral on social media. However, another T-shirt is still being sold in their stores, which says, 'My best subjects are boys, shopping, music and dancing.' When I asked my nine-year-old daughter about her views on these, she said, 'boys have superheroes on their clothes who are strong and powerful, why can't girls be told they have girl power.' She has written a blog titled 'Pretty Clever' on the topic. I wanted a male perspective too so I asked my ten-year-old son for his opinion and his response was interesting. He said: 'The slogans are unfair on both girls and boys because girls are being told they are dumb and they won't learn anything while boys have to do double work!'

Some people will view these slogans as harmless humour – but sleazy and demeaning messages are no joke. Not only do they undermine women's fight for respect and

Too pretty to do maths!

equality, the accumulative effect is damaging. Girls are being prevented from reaching their full potential because they are being conditioned into believing they are not clever and to focus on appearance, boys, and sex. Why are parents buying into these stereotypes? If we don't stop now, the obsession with looks will lead to problems later such as body image dissatisfaction, wanting plastic surgery, eating disorders, low self-esteem and depression. If kids are looking and behaving like mini adults, then they are also more likely to engage in sexual behaviour at an earlier age. It's no wonder that the US has the highest teenage pregnancy rate in the developed world and the UK has the highest rate in Western Europe.

Now that the Government is clamping down on retailers, magazines and broadcasters, we should see less sexualised products and imagery. This will mean less pressure by children on parents. However, recommendations in the Bailey Review on the 'Commercialisation and Sexualisation of Childhood' are only being enforced through voluntary regulations and not legislation. Major British retailers may have signed up to comply but they will always try and constantly push the boundaries.

The only beneficiaries to the sexulisation of children are the corporations and of course paedophiles – after all, sexualisation, whether through adverts, music or products, is a form of grooming. Parents have been helping the very companies that are profiting from the exploitation of their children by buying from them. If we continue then we will be complicit in the sexualisation of our own children. Let's stop right now and not rob them of their childhood.

4 September 2011

⇨ Information from *The Huffington Post*, reprinted with permission from AOL (UK). Please visit www.huffingtonpost.co.uk for further information.

How responsible are women for their sexualisation in the media?

Information from the F word.

By Elin Weiss & Hennie Weiss

A recent article in *Aftonbladet* revealed that the female hockey team the Vancouver Ice-O-Topes are doing a half-naked (and quite highly sexualised) photo shoot in order to financially support their team. Their reason: 'because they love hockey so much'. The Vancouver Ice-O-Topes are, however, not the first team to do so. For example, in 2010 a New Zealand women's rugby team produced a nude calendar in order to draw more women to the sport and to disprove the myth that rugby is 'unfeminine' (implying that a good way to prove one's femininity is to take your clothes off to reveal that your body is in fact feminine, whatever that means). In 2012 the Bristol University netball players also took their clothes off in order to supplement their sponsorship. Other sports-women who have posed in little or no clothing in order to promote themselves include female high jumpers, boxers, swimmers, volleyball players, figure skaters, kayakers, tennis players, and many others. But, the sexualisation of female athletes in calendars and photo shoots does not appear to now be enough. In recent years, an American Lingerie Football League (LFL) has been established in which women play tackle football in their underwear.

We have often thought about how women themselves support the ideals present today by lending themselves to sexualisation. Without women willing to model for highly sexualised or half naked photo shoots, these images would probably not exist. Obviously, not all women perceive the sexualisation of women as a problem, but we feel comfortable stating that many women do feel that the expectations placed on women's appearance and the persistent and rampant sexualisation of women is troublesome, irritating and at times even depressing.

'Should we also stop idolising women who lend themselves to sexualisation?'

The question we as women have to ask ourselves is: How responsible are women for their sexualisation in the media? Can we blame the media, patriarchy, the advertisement companies, and so on without placing some blame, or at least questioning our own involvement in the stereotypical ideals that are presented in the media together with the often highly sexualised and sexist images of women? Should we also stop idolising women who lend themselves to sexualisation and thereby support and encourage these ideals? These are tricky questions to deal with because owning one's involvement in the promotion of sexual ideals of women and a certain appearance is uncomfortable. Women should of course be able to freely express their sexuality. However, do these types of glamour pictures express female sexual empowerment or do they simply provide another method to gain attention or to make money through the sexualisation of women's bodies?

Secondly, how are women's sports ever going to be taken seriously when these women draw attention not to their skills but to their bodies and their appearance? Sure, an underwear calendar is going to draw attention to these teams but the focus will not be on the players and their skills but on which woman is more attractive or how attractive the team is overall. It is true that female athletes often receive fewer endorsements, and less media attention, than male athletes and therefore may look for other venues to increase financial support. Due to the sexualisation of women in our culture, appearing in calendars and photo shoots may be a profitable way to increase revenue. But we have to ask ourselves if the sexualised attention takes away from the credibility of the sport, while depicting female bodies as sex objects rather than strong, competent bodies that deserve attention because of their skills and dedication. How come these talented women resort to nudity and using their bodies in order to promote their sport, which is so unrelated to nudity, appearance and attractiveness? Is taking one's clothes off really female sexual empowerment or is it just another way of gaining popularity through exploitation of the female body since these types of photos are in no way new or inventive, or even aimed at a female audience (despite what the players in the New Zealand rugby team might claim)?

Opinions may differ considerably concerning this issue but we feel that these half-nude shoots are in many ways telling people that nudity and exploitation leads to success and is a good path to explore in order to increase popularity. It becomes a sort of attention-seeking behaviour that is in many ways detrimental to how all women are viewed. It also promotes beliefs in the biological differences between men and women by pointing to women's bodies, not as strong, but as sexual objects that are foremost attractive and sexualised before being competent, strong, fit or successful.

18 March 2012

⇨ Information from the F word. Please visit www.thefword.org.uk for more information.

Readers on ... the sexualisation of girls

A French report has issued guidelines aimed at curbing the hyper-sexualisation of girls. Four readers give their views.

Anonymous

I was first scouted at the age of 14 by one of the world's most prestigious model agencies. I was told that my life had now changed and had to be perfect: bikini waxes, leg waxes, lots of water, perfect skin and having to stay slim were all on the agenda. I had just about started my period by then. When I put on seven pounds to become a whopping seven and a half stone, it was commented on before I'd made it halfway through the office.

I did my first topless shoot a year later for a well-known photographer, and they were photographs that oozed sex. They will tell you that it wouldn't happen in the UK, that it's illegal; I would ask you not to be naive. My father shuddered and wept when he saw them in my model book by accident. He wanted nothing to do with it ever again. I quit modelling at 18 and went to university, tired of seeing my 15- and 16-year-old colleagues on *Vogue* front pages looking like they were all about sex, while overhearing men saying things I couldn't repeat about girls I knew to be still awkward about kissing boys.

'She already, at only three, asks for her nails to be painted and hair to be styled'

As far as I'm concerned we drape paedophilic images from every billboard and expensive magazine. Quite simply a lot of these girls are under 18 and they're made to look 'sexy', 'hot'. These pictures are usually celebrated as high-end culture and something for young girls and women to aspire to. The sexualisation of girls in our culture is rampant and violently damaging, as well as a massive waste of energy and time for girls and women. Isn't it about time that we stopped focusing so much on girls' bodies and outfits and started celebrating their minds and skills?

Lili Owen Rowlands, posts as liliscarlet

In the week in which the inventor of Spanx made this year's world's billionaires list, I flick back through my journal to when, four years ago and aged 15, I described hoisting my own thighs into a pair of the sausage-skin underwear for my school fashion show. 'Hyper-sexualisation' sounds like a stern gynaecologist's description of orgasm and I am hesitant to use it to describe the uneasy feeling I get when I remember my early adolescence, but by 15 I had indeed sexed up my look, perfected a vacuous doe-eyed pout and enslaved myself to the hair-straightener. I am not ashamed of this; nor do I condemn any woman who chooses to flash more than just ankle or curl her eyelashes or paint her nails.

But I am ashamed that I did not question the very notion of sexualisation, that I succumbed to the male gaze so young. Aged 15 I did not realise that stilettos made my feet mimic the shape of a woman's foot in climax. I did not know that my red lipstick resembled the flush of aroused labia. I did not wonder who I was supposed to be pleasing – my male maths partner or myself? My feminism leads me to think that a woman is entirely free to wear whatever she wants: she can show off her legs Monday and wear a turtleneck Tuesday. Nevertheless, it also leads me to think that 'choice' must really be free, and that freedom is rarely felt at 15 when your circulation is being cut off by polyester control pants and your fake eyelashes are jabbing your corneas out.

Melanie Gerlis, posts as melaniegerlis

The sexualisation of young girls is an unfortunate by-product of a modern, western society in which the gulf between the sexes is inexplicably widening. Any efforts to stop this should be welcomed. I have three children, aged three, two and three months. They are a girl, a boy and a girl respectively, and my husband and I have tried, from their births, to bring our two girls and their brother up in an environment that treats them as equals. Despite all efforts, we already feel thwarted by the subtle but incessant drip-feed of sexism that comes not just from books, TV, playgroups and health visitors, but also from family and friends towards our kids. My oldest daughter loves her princess dress, dolls and necklaces because they were gifts to her (my son is the same with his trucks and trains). I know that people find our discomfort extreme – after all, these are generous gifts – and we are much more restrictive than we'd like to be, in order to provide a balance.

A friend who works for a major British clothes designer recently suggested our oldest daughter could model for them. Our initial excitement died down as we realised that this would be an early endorsement of being admired for how she looks, rather than what she does. She already, at only three, asks for her nails to be painted and hair to be styled. These are the things she is routinely 'praised' for and she naturally wants to please. We do what we can to stem the flow, but it wouldn't completely surprise me if she got lingerie for her fourth birthday.

Erinn Dhesi, posts as mrsmiawallace

You cannot mention the hyper-sexualisation of the media without the f-word – feminism. Particularly feminism and its gaping plot holes. At 17, I find that the critics of hyper-sexualisation often mention the 90s as a golden era: 'Oh, we all wore Doc Martens, no make-up and naff clothes and it didn't matter'. Well to paraphrase Kanye West, I'mma let you reminisce about that, but the 90s also brought us third-wave feminism, which allowed us to descend into this vacuous regressive hyper-sexuality. It started with the Spice Girls and *Sex and*

the City and left us having genuine debates on whether vajazzling is a tool of the patriarchy.

It's no coincidence that this topic is brought up while the word feminism is mainly consigned to the blogosphere's murky backwaters: it's an ideology that's dithered, leaving us thinking someone like pop star Rihanna is a 'modern-day feminist' because she dresses sexy and doesn't take orders from anyone (thanks for that, *Cosmopolitan*).

Yes, there is the argument that parents set the tone, but as a teenager you actively seek the opinions of your peers too … and if your peers are huddled around *More* magazine's favourite sexual positions of the week re-enacted by Barbie dolls, you're told to go for the ride because, to quote Gretchen Wieners in *Mean Girls*: 'That's just, like, the rules of feminism!'

11 March 2012

⇨ The above article originally appeared in *The Guardian*. Please visit www.guardian.co.uk for further information.

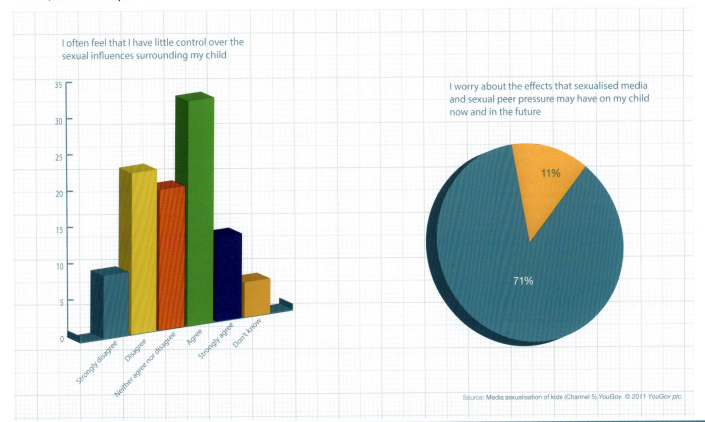

I often feel that I have little control over the sexual influences surrounding my child

I worry about the effects that sexualised media and sexual peer pressure may have on my child now and in the future

11%

71%

Source: Media sexualisation of kids (Channel 5), YouGov. © 2011 YouGov plc.

Key facts

⇨ More than a quarter of 13- to 15-year-olds in the UK have received sexually explicit text messages, while one in ten children aged ten to 12 and a quarter of 13 to 15-year-olds say they have seen sexually explicit images on the Internet, according to a survey for the charities Family Lives and Drinkaware. (page 2)

⇨ The EU Kids Online study earlier this year showed that a quarter of children in the UK aged nine to 16 had seen sexual images in the past 12 months, and 46 per cent of these had seen them online. (page 3)

⇨ 'Young men I have talked to have spoken about the pressure to say that they love pornography and carry it around with them, to have their stock of images on their phone,' Ms Thompson told TESS. 'Young men will say "I have to have my porn, because if I don't, people will call me gay"'. (page 4)

⇨ In 2007, a study by the American Psychological Association found that: 'Sexualisation has negative effects in a variety of domains, including physical and mental health, and healthy sexual development.' (page 9)

⇨ A 2008 study by Girlguiding UK and the Mental Health Foundation found that premature sexualisation and pressure to grow up too quickly are two 'key influences' in the anxiety felt by girls. (page 9)

⇨ Evidence gathered in the Home Office review on sexualisation suggests a clear link between consumption of sexualised images, tendency to view women as objects and the acceptance of aggressive attitudes and behaviour as the norm. (page 11)

⇨ 25% of UK children aged eight to 12 have smartphones, and more than one in five of those children admitted to accessing websites that they know are 'not for them.' (page 19)

⇨ The number of children watching 'online videos or video clips' on their mobile phones has more than doubled from 15% in 2008 to 36% in 2011. (page 19)

⇨ 74% think warnings and ratings would help protect children from content that they should perhaps not be looking at. (page 20)

⇨ Shockingly, six out of ten parents do not feel able to protect their children from inappropriate images in music videos and DVDs. While 18% make sure every video their children watch is suitable, 46% say they try to monitor what their children watch but can't be with them all the time. A further 16% admit they can't stop them watching videos as they are so easily available. (page 20)

⇨ 62% of parents that we surveyed think currently lyrics in songs are too sexually explicit. (page 20)

⇨ The majority [of parents] (43%) think children would find ways to watch the videos regardless of what restrictions the government attempted to put in place. (page 20)

⇨ Recent research from Plymouth University reveals that 40 per cent of 14- to 16-year-olds say they have friends who have engaged in sexting. Even more worrying, 20 per cent expressed that there was nothing wrong with full nudity in such messages, while 40 per cent said topless pictures were acceptable. (page 23)

⇨ Starting in 2012, all four leading Internet service providers (BT, Sky, TalkTalk and Virgin) will make sure that anyone signing up to a new broadband deal will have to choose whether or not they want to turn on parental control software, so that access to certain websites is blocked. (page 25)

⇨ 83% of adults said they didn't think beauty pageants should be available for girls of this age and 86% of respondents said they wouldn't let their daughter (aged 13 or under) in such a competition even if there was appropriate monitoring and security. (page 29)

⇨ The majority of adults think the pageants are just too risky (78%) with the top three concerns being sexualisation of children (82%), obsessive/pushy parents (81%) and paedophile interest (72%). (page 29)

⇨ Nine in ten parents (90%) still think there are problems with the way some companies advertise to children and 85% are unaware of the dedicated complaints and advice website ParentPort, according to a poll for the Chartered Institute of Marketing (CIM). (page 35)

Androgynous

Gender neutral, as opposed to appearing strictly male or female. Androgyny usually implies a blend of both feminine and masculine attributes.

Beauty pageant

Beauty pageants are generally aimed at females (though similar events do exist for males). Contestants are judged on the combined criteria of physical beauty, personality and talent. There is, however, a tendency to focus on physical appearance above other characteristics. Some feel that beauty pageants are inappropriate for young girls because they promote a nation obsessed with looks. On the other hand, some believe that pageants promote confidence and self-esteem.

Commercial/Commercialisation

Exploiting something in order to gain money.

Gender stereotypes

Simplifying the roles, attributes and differences between males and females. Gender stereotyping encourages children to behave in ways that are considered most typical of their sex. For example, buying pink toys for girls and blue for boys, or limiting girls to playing with dolls and boys to toy-cars.

Grooming

Today, grooming is increasingly carried out via the Internet and is usually conducted by an adult, towards a child or teenager. The 'groomer' deliberately befriends a child and lures them into a false sense of security by establishing an emotional connection (this might involve pretending to have similar interests, or being sympathetic towards their problems). When this false friendship is established, the 'groomer' then begins to coax the child into sending them sexual images or performing sexual acts.

Hypermasculinity

Hypermasculinity refers to stereotypical male behaviour, with an emphasis on physical aggression and strength. Hypermasculine traits include: violence, aggressive sexual behaviour and a derogatory attitude towards women. Viewing material such as pornography, in which these traits are exaggerated, can lead to young men believing they should display these characteristics or behaviours.

Parental control software/Network-level filters

Parental control software makes use of web filters to block access to certain websites that contain inappropriate content for minors. This includes websites about suicide/self-harm, gambling, file sharing and pornography. Net-filters provide parents with the option of blocking adult content, such as porn, and placing certain websites on a 'black list' so that they cannot be accessed. In 2012, the four leading Internet service providers in the UK (BT, Sky, TalkTalk and Virgin) will offer new customers the choice of whether or not they want to turn on parental control software.

Pornification

Very similar to sexualisation, the term pornification refers to the acceptance of sexualisation in our culture.

'Safetynet' petition

The 'Safetynet' petition, which has been signed by 110,000 people including peers, MPs and religious figures, asks Internet service providers such as BT, Sky and Virgin to cut off access to adult content on computers and mobile phones. The aim is to block access to hardcore pornography by default and people will have to 'opt-in' to view adult sites.

Sexualise/Sexualisation

To give someone or something sexual characteristics and associations. This refers to the idea that sex has become much more visible in culture and media today. Premature sexualisation of children involves exposure to sexual images and ideas at an age when they are emotionally unable to process such information. Implications include children having sex at a younger age, engaging in activities such as sexting, an increased likelihood of being groomed and has been linked to hypermasculine behaviour in boys and young men.

Watershed restrictions

A television watershed is in place to protect children from viewing material that is inappropriate for their age group. Adult content can only be shown after a certain time (or 'after the watershed'). Some examples of adult content include graphic violence, nudity, swearing, gambling and drug use. Watershed times can vary around the world due to cultural difference. For example, in the UK the watershed for free-to-air television is between 21:00 and 05:30, whereas in the United states it begins at 22:00 and ends at 06:00.

Assignments

1. Using the articles in Chapter 1 as a starting point, write your own definition of the term 'sexualisation'. When you have finished, split into small groups and discuss your definitions. Feed back to the rest of the class.

2. Read the article 'Letting children be children' on page five. Do you agree with the recommendations that are made in the report? Are there any that you consider unrealistic or unachievable? Write a one page summary of your opinions, focussing on anything you strongly disagree with.

3. Read 'Let Girls Be Girls...' on pages eight and nine. The article talks about Mumsnet's campaign to stop retailers selling 'equalised products aimed at children' and describes the effects of premature sexualisation on girls. What about boys? What is the effect of, for example, lads magazines such as Nuts or Zoo on young boys? Discuss with a partner, and then write a paragraph summarising your thoughts.

4. Why do you think the premature sexualisation of girls could lead to increased domestic violence against women? Discuss in small groups and feed back to the rest of the class.

5. Visit your local toy shop, or look at the children's section of an online retailer. Are there any products you feel are inappropriate for young children? Write a report for your local newspaper, highlighting your findings. Maybe you feel that there aren't any toys that are inappropriate – in this case you could argue that premature sexualisation has been 'hyped' up by the media.

6. Choose one of the illustrations from the book and consider what message your chosen picture is trying to get across. How does it support, or add to, the points made in the accompanying article? Do you think it is successful?

7. 'Digital and communication technologies are opening up children to new practices and pressures at a rate which leaves both parents and children struggling to fully recognise the potential risks and implications for the future. It is imperative that the ways in which children make use of new technology is known to parents...' (page 15). Design a leaflet explaining the new technology that children use, to parents who might be unaware of the risks. For example, your leaflet could consider social media and privacy settings, smartphone technology, YouTube, Skype and other platforms that could enable 'sexual exploitation, harassment and bullying'.

8. Design a questionnaire that will be distributed throughout your school and filled in anonymously. The questionnaire should aim to discover how much 'inappropriate material' is viewed online by young people of different ages. You should consider what should be classed as 'inappropriate material', how young people are accessing this material, what effect it has on them and what they think should be done about it. To take this further, you could discuss your questionnaires as a class and come up with a final list that will be distributed throughout the school so you can analyse the results.

9. Do you think that music videos should be given age-ratings, the same way that DVDs are? Write a blog post justifying your opinion.

10. Read the articles that discuss the sexualised nature of music videos on pages 20 – 22. Choose a song that is currently in the music charts, and draw a story board for a new music video that would be appropriate for all age groups.

11. Read the article "Sexting" may be just a normal part of dating for Internet generation' on page 24. Do you agree with the idea that sexting is a 'normal, healthy component of modern dating'? What are the dangers involved in sexting?

12. Imagine that you are the parent of a six-year-old girl. One of her friends is being entered into a local child beauty pageant, and your daughter decides she wants to take part too. Would you let your daughter enter the beauty pageant? Discuss in small groups.

13. Write a three page report, answering the following question: 'How responsible are parents for the sexualisation of children in today's society?' Use the articles from Chapter 3 as a starting point.

14. Look at the pie-chart titled 'Things haven't changed with the sexualisation of children and people just exaggerate how much things have changed' on page 34. Do some research into the kinds of music videos, magazines and toys that were available when your parents were growing up. Compare this with what you know about today's society. Do you think people exaggerate how much things have changed? Create a PowerPoint presentation to demonstrate your point of view, using images, video, newspapers etc. to help.

Acknowledgements

The publisher is grateful for permission to reproduce the following material.

While every care has been taken to trace and acknowledge copyright, the publisher tenders its apology for any accidental infringement or where copyright has proved untraceable. The publisher would be pleased to come to a suitable arrangement in any such case with the rightful owner.

Chapter One: What is sexualisation?

Pleasure vs profit © Women's Support Project, War against the sexualisation of childhood © 2012 TSL Education, Letting children be children © Crown copyright 2011, Let Girls Be Girls campaign © Mumsnet Limited, Review into sexualisation of young people published © PSHE Association, The Home Office report on child sexualisation is a 100-page Cosmopolitan article © Telegraph Media Group Limited 2010, Sexualised wallpaper © NHS Sheffield, All of our concern: commercialisation, sexualisation and hypermasculinity © Family Lives.

Chapter Two: The impact of porn

Sexualisation of children - protecting innocence online © 2012 AOL (UK) Limited, Hidden tide of child-on-child sex attacks © Telegraph Media Group Limited 2012, Ex 'lads' mag' editor: I regret my part in normalising porn © The Christian Institute, Over one in five UK Children view 'inappropriate content' on their smartphones © Carphone Warehouse Group PLC 2012, Parents feel unable to protect children from inappropriate images © OnePoll 2012, A lack of clothes is not the problem with music videos today © Guardian News & Media Ltd 2012, X Factor judge says music videos are too sexualised © The Christian Institute, Teenage sexting © 2011 Barnevakten and KidsOKOnline, 'Sexting may be just a normal part of dating for Internet generation' © University of Michigan 2012, Web Providers offer parents option to block porn © 2011 Barnevakten and KidsOKOnline, Internet porn petition will reach the Government with 100, 000 signatures © 2012 AOL (UK) Limited.

Chapter Two: Debating sexualisation

French report calls for end to sexualisation of children © Guardian News & Media Ltd 2012, Mum dresses toddler up as a prostitute for beauty pageant © 2012 AOL (UK) Limited, UK beauty pageant for girls under 13 branded 'pointless' and 'tacky'... © OnePoll 2012, Child beauty shows? They're harmless fun blasts mum Gemma Blackhurst © MEN Media 2012, Fury over Primark's padded bikinis for children © 2010 Press Association, Hot pants or hot air? © the F word, Sexualisation of childhood: Facebook and padded bras worry 90% of parents © 2012 Press Association, Parents becoming complicit in the sexualisation of children © 2012 AOL (UK) Limited, How responsible are women for their sexualisation in the media? © the F word, Readers on ... the sexualisation of girls © Guardian News & Media Ltd 2012.

Illustrations:

Pages 23 & 30: Don Hatcher, pages 17 & 28: Simon Kneebone, pages 6 & 26, Angelo Madrid.

Images:

Cover and page 27: © s-dmit, page 3 © Jeff Osborn; page 12 © iconogenic, page 19 © Osman Kalkavan, page 21 © Gabriella Fabbri, page 25 © Shane Link, page 32 © 07_av, page 35 © paci77, page 36 © Michaela Steininger.

Additional acknowledgements:

Editorial on behalf of Independence Educational Publishers by Cara Acred.
With thanks to the Independence team: Mary Chapman, Sandra Dennis, Christina Hughes, Jackie Staines and Jan Sunderland.

Cara Acred
Cambridge, January 2013